"In the ancient Mediterranean, 'fathers' were always superior to 'sons.' In some ancient Jewish traditions, a messiah might be divine, but he was the lieutenant, not the equal, of the supreme power, the God of Israel. By 325 CE, however, the Council of Nicaea would pronounce Christ equal in divinity to God. How, and when, did this mutation in monotheism occur? Does christological divinity—Christ as *a* god—imply divine identity, Christ *as* God? Ehrman and Bird debate all these issues with erudition and lively good humor. When did Jesus become God? Great question—with myriad different answers."
  —Paula Fredriksen, Aurelio Professor Emerita of Scripture,
     Boston University, and Distinguished Visiting Professor,
                    the Hebrew University of Jerusalem

"A reader may come to this book already knowing which side is correct, and I was no exception; but that did not prevent me from thoroughly enjoying the book—I enjoyed reading it more than I ever thought I would. In a world that is increasingly polarized, it is more important than ever to have—and model—respectful dialogue, debate, and disagreement. This book is important because it is both an introduction to an ongoing scholarly debate and also an example of how to argue well. The opening section on historiological methodology alone would make this book invaluable. From now on, when I teach historiography, I will assign this book."
  —James L. Papandrea, Professor of Church
              History and Historical Theology,
         Garrett-Evangelical Theological Seminary

T0278178

"Although there are many reasons to recommend *When Did Jesus Become God?*, I can cite three that identify this as an essential, short model for Christian debate: Stewart's clear articulation of a user-friendly approach to historical analysis; the irenic and respectful interaction of Ehrman and Bird, which is sincerely lacking in much modern discourse; and the clear dialogic approach to a theology that is at the core of Christian faith. Get this book!"

—Jacquelyn E. Winston, Professor Emerita of Church History and Theology, Azusa Pacific University

"It's not every day that you find a debate about *when* early Christians believed Jesus was divine prefaced by a very helpful introductory discussion of logic and how to assess historical arguments. But that, in fact, is what we find in this extremely interesting little book. The focus in the book is not on Jesus' self-understanding but on what the earliest Christians believed about Jesus after his death and resurrection. The lively but respectful and humorous back-and-forth between Michael Bird and Bart Ehrman is worth the price of the book all by itself."

—Ben Witherington III, Jean R. Amos Professor of New Testament for Doctoral Studies, Asbury Theological Seminary

When Did Jesus Become God?

When Did Jesus Become God?

A Christological Debate

BART D. EHRMAN
MICHAEL F. BIRD
AND
ROBERT B. STEWART

 WESTMINSTER
JOHN KNOX PRESS
LOUISVILLE • KENTUCKY

First edition
Published by Westminster John Knox Press
Louisville, Kentucky

22 23 24 25 26 27 28 29 30 31—10 9 8 7 6 5 4 3 2 1

Book design by Drew Stevens
Cover design by Marc Whitaker / MTWdesign.net

Library of Congress Cataloging-in-Publication Data

Names: Ehrman, Bart D., author. | Bird, Michael F., author. | Stewart, Robert B., 1957– author.
Title: When did Jesus become God? : a christological debate / Bart D. Ehrman, Michael F. Bird, and Robert B. Stewart.
Description: First edition. | Louisville, Kentucky : Westminster John Knox Press, [2022] | Includes bibliographical references and index. | Summary: "How did early Christians come to believe that Jesus of Nazareth was the divine Son of God? This is the central question in this transcribed conversation between Bart Ehrman and Michael Bird, with a historiographic introduction by Robert Stewart that helps readers understand the conclusions reached by Ehrman and Bird"—Provided by publisher.
Identifiers: LCCN 2022033362 (print) | LCCN 2022033363 (ebook) | ISBN 9780664265861 (paperback) | ISBN 9781646982844 (ebook)
Subjects: LCSH: Jesus Christ—Divinity—History of doctrines—Early church, ca. 30–600.
Classification: LCC BT216.3 .E39 2022 (print) | LCC BT216.3 (ebook) | DDC 232/.8—dc23/eng/20220909
LC record available at https://lccn.loc.gov/2022033362
LC ebook record available at https://lccn.loc.gov/2022033363

In memory of

Larry Hurtado

Jesus' earliest followers believed he had been taken up into heaven. What were they supposed to think about that? They thought what anybody at the time would think: he had been made a divine being. And so, the earliest christological views— the earliest views of who Christ was—were that at the resurrection, God made Jesus a divine being. It was at the resurrection that Jesus became the Son of God.

—Bart Ehrman

Certainly, if you read a passage like Acts 13:33–34, there is exaltation language [meaning], "This man Jesus has been exalted to divine status." We face questions: Is that all they believed? Was that the limits of their belief? Do they compact everything around that? Do they believe nothing more? . . . Would they have concluded that he was enthroned with Yahweh, that we should now use the language of Isaiah 45 to describe him, that he held life and power, redemption, and the majesty of God in his hands? I don't think so.

—Michael Bird

The primary reason a historian should believe that Jesus was aware of his divine identity is the number and variety of ways he demonstrated an awareness that he possessed an authority equal to that of Israel's God. He acted in word and deed in ways in which only Israel's God had authority to act.

—Robert Stewart

Contents

Acknowledgments

Thanking others in print is always an occasion for anxiety because of the fear that some who deserve a word of appreciation will be overlooked through human error. But many deserve to be publicly thanked, and even praised, so we must go on. The dialogue that is featured in this book came from the twelfth Greer-Heard Point-Counterpoint Forum.[1] So, first of all, we must thank Bill and Carolyn Heard for their passion to have a forum where leading scholars can dialogue about important issues in faith and culture in a collegial manner and on a balanced playing field. Without them the Greer-Heard Point-Counterpoint Forum in Faith and Culture would be a dream rather than a reality.

The event would never have taken place without the efforts of Emily Sloane Jarrell and her staff at the Providence Learning Center of NOBTS. Vanee Daure and the media staff of NOBTS must also be thanked for recording it in both audio and video formats.

The dialogue was initially transcribed by Bryan Shuler. He deserves a word of thanks not only for the transcription but also for carrying out other tasks related to the project flawlessly and with enthusiasm. Ricky Michalski and Micah Chung also need to be thanked for their assistance in research and with details of the project in its final stages. Micah also prepared the index for publication. Concerning various topics related to the subject of this book, Robert Stewart is also grateful for fruitful

---

1. The Greer-Heard Point-Counterpoint Forum was a five-year pilot project of New Orleans Baptist Theological Seminary (NOBTS) that began in 2005. The Forum was made possible by a generous gift from donors Bill and Carolyn Greer Heard; the forum was named in honor of their parents. Apparently they were pleased with the results from that initial five-year trial because in total there were fourteen Greer-Heard Point-Counterpoint Forums.

communication with Chuck Quarles, Bill Warren, Dan Wallace, Mike Licona, and Rob Bowman.

We very much appreciate Daniel Braden at Westminster John Knox for his interest in publishing this volume as well as his enthusiasm for fair-minded, respectful dialogue on important issues. Additionally, he was always timely in responding to questions and a source of much good advice and encouragement.

Our wives and family must also be thanked; they are consistent sources of support. No book such as this ever is written apart from the scholars who have gone before us. In particular, we are grateful to Larry W. Hurtado, whose groundbreaking work we all applaud. Larry was a magnificent scholar and perhaps even a better human being. It is to him that we dedicate this book.

Judging What They Say about Jesus

Instructions for Assessing Historical Arguments

ROBERT B. STEWART

My father was a judge, which makes me a JK, a judge's kid! Growing up as a JK is not easy. Having a judge as a father is like living with a human lie detector. A constant refrain in our home was "Boys, I hear better liars than you every day." My dad was a skeptic; he did not simply take us at our word, but examined everything we said in light of the available evidence to see whether what we told him was plausible or implausible. What we told him had to be believable and coherent: it had to make sense in light of everything else that he knew. As a judge my father was a student of human nature and knew that we are all inclined to try to make ourselves look as good as possible by whatever means possible. So he was always on guard, making it difficult for us to pull the wool over his eyes. Not only was it difficult to deceive him, but when we were found guilty—and especially when we perjured ourselves to cover up our peccadillos—our father sentenced us to pay for those misdeeds.[1]

---

1. Because my father was a competitive skeet shooter, the most common form of punishment was reloading shotgun shells. Reloading shotgun shells was a worse form of punishment than it sounds like. The reloading machines for the different gauges of shotguns used in skeet shooting were in the garage, which meant no air conditioning in the summer and no heater in the winter. To top that off, reloading

One of the things for which my father was frequently applauded was the way he would instruct those involved in trials, whether they were jurors or defendants, as to what was going on in a trial and what their rights and responsibilities were. One tribute to him after his death quoted him as saying, "I have always tried to make people understand what is going on in their case. If we are to serve our function of changing people's conduct, how are they going to be changed if they don't know what happened to them?"[2]

Why do I mention this? Because in some ways historians are like jurors.[3] *Both jurors and historians are concerned with discovering the truth about the past.* And to do their jobs effectively, both jurors and historians need to adhere to certain well-reasoned guidelines. In some ways, readers are in a similar position. Good readers critically judge the theses (arguments) that are brought before them. Therefore, my intention in this essay is to offer readers some instructions as to how to assess a historical case.

PRELIMINARY INSTRUCTIONS

Understand the hypothesis that is presented. This *seems* so obvious that it shouldn't need to be stated. But because most readers are impatient, they sometimes take mental shortcuts; as a result, they miss important details that they might otherwise recognize. When readers don't fully understand a hypothesis, they are dealing with something other than what is actually proposed and thus critiquing something other than what has actually been proposed. Therefore, before one can make a historical judgment about a hypothesis, one must understand what that hypothesis actually is.

---

shotgun shells is a mindless, repetitive task—which gave my brother and me time to think about what we had done to put ourselves in this situation. So maybe it served its purpose.

2. Mark White, "Judge Blaine Stewart was a great man, who will be missed," *News Journal*, April 7, 2021, https://www.thenewsjournal.net/judge-blaine-stewart-was-a-great-man-who-will-be-missed/.

3. By "juror" I mean either a member of a jury or a judge; I am not contrasting a jury member to the judge. In many trials there is no jury; when there is no jury, the judge is the sole juror, a jury of one. In no trial is there no juror.

Be charitable when assessing a hypothesis or an argument. The principle of charity states that we should seek to "maximize the soundness of others' arguments and truth of their claims by rendering them in the strongest way reasonable."[4] When there are two or more possible ways to understand a hypothesis, we should understand it in the way that is most rational and persuasive within its context, all other things being equal. We should not resort to accusations of bias or shortsightedness before exhausting other options. We also need to keep in mind that even though an overall hypothesis may be incorrect, there may be points at which it is correct and helpful. The principle of charity is one of the first things one learns in philosophy, but the principle applies to other fields as well. Being charitable means that in seeking to understand a hypothesis, historians need to take it in its best possible light, recognizing that even if poorly stated, it may be fundamentally correct, or at least have a grain of truth in it. It also means that sometimes the historian needs to strengthen the argument or refine the hypothesis under consideration to address the fundamental issue properly. One idea that undergirds the principle of charity is that if one has dealt with the best argument for a position and found it wanting, then all the lesser expressions of it fail as well. Besides the obvious logical concern behind the principle of charity, there is also a hermeneutical end. Historians should focus on *what is meant* rather than merely upon *what is said.* Additionally, there is an ethical concern, namely, the Golden Rule. We should treat others and their ideas as we want them to treat us and our ideas.

Judge a hypothesis from start to finish. It's always tempting to skip to the end of the book. Historians must resist the temptation to peek at the conclusion of a historical argument, and if they agree with its conclusion, simply accept it without critically assessing the steps it takes and the reasoning employed to reach its conclusion. Nor should any historian approach an argument with a bias toward the person who made it. Facts are stubborn things; the truth value of a statement doesn't depend upon who

4. Julian Baggini and Peter S. Fosl, *The Philosopher's Toolkit* (Malden, MA: Wiley-Blackwell, 2010), 115.

utters it. All historians must first consider the available evidence and assess the reasoning used to reach the conclusion before affirming or rejecting any argument or historical hypothesis.

There is a difference between the evidence and your opinion concerning the evidence. I frequently point out to my students that there is a difference between the Bible and their interpretation of the Bible (whatever view they take regarding the Bible's trustworthiness). This hermeneutical principle also applies to history. Good historians approach historical questions with an attitude of humility. We could be wrong. I know that *I have been wrong at some point* because I have changed my mind on any number of matters, both hermeneutical and historical. Either I was wrong in the past but am now right, or I was right in the past but am now wrong, or I was wrong in the past and I am still wrong, but wrong in a different way or for different reasons. The one thing that cannot be the case is that I have always been right! I do my best. I critically assess what I believe. I tenaciously hold to my beliefs (some more tenaciously than others) and do not abandon them unless I am persuaded that other beliefs are more rational. But I do all this with epistemological humility, understanding that I have an intellectual and moral responsibility to fairly consider the viewpoints of others, especially those with whom I presently disagree.

Historical conclusions can be revised. Unlike jurors, who render binding legal verdicts, historians can change their conclusions. A legal verdict may be overturned; if it is, it will not be done by the person or persons who rendered the initial verdict, but by a higher court. Historians, however, can always revise their beliefs, and sometimes they should.

History proceeds on the basis of inferences. Historians infer conclusions about historical figures or events from the evidence they have at their disposal. This means that two or more historians may argue for contrary positions by appealing to the same evidence. Frequently the debate is over *what the evidence means* rather than over what evidence is relevant, although historians also make inferences in determining what evidence is relevant. Ultimately historians tell an explanatory story intended to make sense of the relevant evidence. These explanatory stories are drawn from the inferences they make concerning the evidence. Earlier inferences lead to conclusions, or subconclusions, from which they draw further inferences, and thus reach other conclusions.

An argument or a hypothesis is not evidence. An argument may be based upon evidence—most arguments are to one degree or another—but there is a difference between an argument and evidence. Arguments reveal what one takes the evidence to show. Arguments also serve as pleas for others to agree with our position as to what the evidence means. But evidence is one thing; arguments are another.

What should be evident by now is the fact that there is such a thing as historical truth, though this is denied by many today. Some maintain that history is simply a cultural construct. But once we speak more clearly as to what we mean by history, much of the confusion can be cleared away. We must distinguish between *history as an event in the past* (History-E) and *history as what is written about select events in the past* (History-W). Historians tell stories about the past, which they believe to have History-E as the focal point of the story, chronological ground zero, if you will. Modern historians cannot observe History-E directly. Nor can they reflect on their feelings about the event as the event is unfolding, as ancient observers could and often did. Our access to the specific content of the past is generally through History-W, the stories that ancient writers told. So there is a sense in which writers in antiquity, by interpreting and shaping the story as they did, constructed the history that is available to us today.

The fact that History-W is in this sense constructed does not mean that all historical opinions are equally true. All History-W is shaped by several things: (1) *The selection by the historian.* No historian includes everything known about any historical figure or event. Instead, historians write about events and relationships in the lives of historical persons that they consider significant. (2) *The perspective of the historian.* For example, how a historian writes about the Cold War depends on whether one is a Soviet or an American. (3) *The historian's understanding of what the biblical authors meant by what they wrote.* For example, did Paul in Philippians 2:6 mean that Jesus' nature was one of equality with God the Father *or* that Jesus had the status of a lesser deity?[5] (4) *The worldview of the historian.* The worldview of the historian is perhaps the most important aspect of all because our worldviews shape and color how we view reality. If a historian has a naturalist worldview, then that historian will first seek natural explanations for purported miracles and perhaps not even consider a supernatural explanation. If one has a determinist worldview, then one will place less emphasis upon human intention in the analysis of why historical figures acted as they did. To a significant degree worldviews limit the range of explanation that a historian is open to believing. But worldviews are not strictly determinative. Individuals can, and often do, critique their own worldviews, and some change worldviews as a result.[6] We all have a worldview even if we don't know what a worldview is. A worldview can enhance or inhibit the historian's search for truth.

All this highlights the fact that *there is always a hermeneutical dimension to historical writing.* All historical writing obviously involves a process of selection (one event or person is written about while another is not). What is not as readily apparent is that selecting entails a process of interpretation because what is selected is determined on the basis of what is deemed meaningful, and meaning is a hermeneutical issue. Clearly, then, interpretation (hermeneutics) is as much a part of writing history as it is of reading history. Historians write about history as interpretation in a way that does not exclude history as "real events in the past." In other words, History-W refers to History-E, *objective events* in the past, *through interpretation,*

5. Phil. 2:6: "who, though he was in the form of God, did not regard equality with God as something to be exploited" (NRSV); ὃς ἐν μορφῇ θεοῦ ὑπάρχων οὐχ ἁρπαγμὸν ἡγήσατο τὸ εἶναι ἴσα θεῷ (Greek New Testament).

6. For instance, both Bart Ehrman and Michael Bird have had a change in worldviews, Ehrman from conservative Christian to agnostic, and Bird from atheist to Christian. For more on how worldviews impact the writing and reading of history, see N. T. Wright, *The New Testament and the People of God*, vol. 1, *Christian Origins and the Question of God* (Minneapolis: Fortress Press, 1992), 38–88, esp. 83–88.

not apart from interpretation. N. T. Wright states it thus: "The myth of uninterpreted history functions precisely as a myth in much modern discourse—that is, it expresses an ideal state of affairs which we imagine erroneously to exist, and which influences the way we think and speak. But it is a 'myth,' in the popular sense, for all that."[7] None of this means that there is no truth to matters of the past, or that all historical writing is simply a matter of perspective. History is, of course, a matter of perspective, but it is not *merely* a matter of perspective. For instance, either Nixon knew about the Watergate cover-up, or he did not. Either Jesus was buried after he was crucified, or he was not. The perspectival nature of history does nothing to mitigate the laws of noncontradiction and excluded middle.

Because historians are the gatekeepers, we must not only be aware of the agendas of historical figures but also of the agendas of the historians writing about them. For example, both Ann Coulter[8] and George Stephanopoulos[9] have written books about the Clinton White House. Both Coulter and Stephanopoulos have agendas; their agendas are not remotely similar. In the same way, one should understand the perspectives of ancient historians and modern historians writing about the ancient world. In fact, knowledge of the agenda of a historical figure may increase the historian's ability to know the truth.

Our certainty that we know the truth about the past is never on the same level as the certainty we can have about mathematics, but that doesn't mean that there is no truth to historical claims, or even that we can't know that truth. We simply know what we know with less than 100 percent logical certainty. But *we don't have 100 percent logical certainty concerning most of what we know*. In fact, we don't have absolute certainty about most of our most important beliefs. We routinely base our existential commitments on beliefs about which we cannot be logically certain. We routinely travel in cars and planes with

7. Wright, *New Testament and the People of God*, 1:85.
8. Ann Coulter, *High Crimes and Misdemeanors: The Case against Bill Clinton* (Washington, DC: Regnery Publishing, 1998).
9. George Stephanopoulos, *All Too Human: A Political Education* (Boston: Little, Brown & Co., 1999).

less than 100 percent certainty that we will safely arrive at our destinations. Perhaps a story will illustrate.

Several years ago one of my colleagues asked me to join him and his college-age son for lunch because his son was going through a crisis of faith. The young man had been raised in a Christian home, attended Bible-believing churches, and was frequently exposed to the best Christian theology. Nevertheless, he was genuinely doubting the foundation of the Christian faith. We went to lunch, and I began to ask him questions as to where he was in his faith and why. (Note: I did not assume that I knew why he was doubting. I wanted to hear him in his own words.) Rather quickly, I thought I had identified his basic issue. The conversation that followed went like this:

STEWART   If I'm understanding you, you think that there's rather good evidence for the existence of God, the truthfulness of Christianity, and the resurrection of Jesus, but you're troubled because you can't be 100 percent certain that these things are true, yet Christianity calls for a 100 percent commitment of your life. Am I understanding you correctly? (*Notice again: I made certain that I was actually addressing his issue, not simply repeating a stock apologetic answer!*)

YOUTH   Yes, exactly.

STEWART   Do you want to get married?

YOUTH   *looking somewhat confused.* Oh yeah, I'm going to get married.

STEWART   OK. When you get married, would you like to have a wife who is faithful to you 100 percent of the time, or would it be OK if she cheated on you occasionally, like once every leap year?

YOUTH   I want a wife who is always faithful to me!

STEWART   But how could you ever be certain that she was faithful to you 100 percent of the time?

YOUTH   *after a long pause.* I guess I couldn't be 100 percent certain.

STEWART   So I guess you're never going to get married.
YOUTH   I'm going to get married.
STEWART   But you can't be certain.
YOUTH   I'm going to get married.
STEWART   But marriage—just like Christianity—requires
          a total, 100 percent commitment of your life,
          and you've already agreed that you can't be cer-
          tain that your future wife will always be faithful
          to you.

At that moment the lightbulb came on as the realization hit
him that even our most important existential commitments
don't require 100 percent logical certainty. So it is with historical knowledge. We can know vitally important facts about the
past without having 100 percent certainty as to their truthfulness.[10] We can even base our lives on beliefs about the past that
we are not 100 percent certain about!

In fact, we hold some logically uncertain yet crucially important beliefs so tightly that we cannot *not* believe them. For
instance, I cannot disbelieve that my wife will love me tomorrow. I know that she *can* choose not to love me tomorrow, but
it is impossible for me to actually believe that she *will* not love
me tomorrow. How can I be so certain? One word: evidence!
I have abundant evidence, accumulated for over thirty-eight
years on a daily basis and in multiple ways, that my wife loves
me and will continue to love me for better or for worse, for
richer or for poorer, in sickness and in health, until one of us
dies. I have more than enough evidence to convince me that
she is the sort of person who will love me tomorrow because I
know her to have the strength of character to keep her vows.
At some point the cumulative effect of this sustained barrage
of evidence overwhelms even my professionally trained level
of skepticism. All this points out not only that we can know

---

10. Sometimes one hears, "Extraordinary claims require extraordinary evidence." This is simply not
true. The evidence for some claims is extraordinary, but no belief requires extraordinary evidence (as
though what it would mean for evidence to be "extraordinary" were obvious). Beliefs require sufficient
evidence, justification, or warrant. The distinctions between evidence, justification, and warrant need
not detain us here.

vitally important facts without 100 percent logical certainty, but also that historical knowledge, like most of our knowledge, is arrived at by an a posteriori rather an a priori manner.

I am not saying that we do not need to examine relevant evidence when and if it is brought forward to challenge our beliefs. I am also not saying that we shouldn't examine the arguments that support our own beliefs to assess their merits. We should be as skeptical about our skepticism as we are about the beliefs of those with whom we disagree. But I am saying that somebody else having a different opinion on a matter than I do is not the sort of evidence needed to defeat a properly based historical belief. It is evidence that someone disagrees with me: that's all. It is not the kind of evidence needed to change my mind, nor is it proof that our contrary views are equally correct or incorrect.

DEFEATERS

A "defeater" is a reason either to change your belief as to the truth value of a statement, or to doubt what you previously believed about a statement. There are different types of defeaters. For our purposes, two types of defeaters are relevant: *undercutting* defeaters and *rebutting* defeaters. An undercutting defeater is the sort of evidence that undermines my confidence in my belief concerning a particular proposition. On the other hand, a rebutting defeater is evidence that changes my belief concerning a particular proposition either from belief to unbelief or from unbelief to belief. A rebutting defeater is thus stronger than an undercutting defeater because a rebutting defeater makes it irrational for me to continue to believe what I had previously believed.

Perhaps some hypothetical examples will illustrate the difference between these two types of defeaters.

Example #1: When I left the house this morning, my wife had a slight headache but assured me that otherwise she was feeling fine. As a result, I came to believe that my wife was well. Later my wife called and told me that she had been to the doctor because she had developed a sore throat and had begun to run a fever, and a test had confirmed that she had strep throat. I no longer believe that my wife is well. In fact, I form a contradictory belief: I now believe that my wife is ill. *The call from my wife served as a rebutting defeater* for my earlier belief that my wife was well. After hearing that she had tested positive for strep throat, it became impossible for me to believe that she was well.

Example #2: This morning I glanced out my office window onto the Quad of our seminary and saw what appeared to be people dressed like faeries prancing about on the lawn of the Quad. This was admittedly unusual, but I generally trust my eyesight unless given a reason to doubt it. So although I was puzzled, I concluded that I was in fact seeing faeries. Ten minutes later, I received an email addressed to faculty and staff saying that around the time that I thought I was seeing faeries, a leaky tanker truck carrying a hallucinogenic gas drove past my office. The email encouraged us to report to the campus clinic if we began to see strange things. *The email served as an undercutting defeater* for my belief that this morning there were faeries in the Quad. I do not know *for certain* that I inhaled any of the gas or that I was hallucinating, but I do not need to know for certain that I was hallucinating for my confidence in my belief concerning faeries to be undercut.

Undercutting defeaters are thus weaker than rebutting defeaters. Whereas rebutting defeaters have the power to change my belief about a proposition from belief to unbelief, or vice versa, undercutting defeaters merely have the power to cause me to be uncertain about my belief concerning a proposition. Yet both are significant.

But defeaters can be defeated. Suppose that right before I left for the clinic (because I had seen something strange on the Quad), I read an email sent even earlier that morning to faculty informing us that a troupe of Shakespearian actors would be rehearsing *A Midsummer Night's Dream* in the Quad that morning. That would serve to defeat the undercutting defeater to my belief that faeries were dancing on the Quad. I conclude that I indeed see people dressed like faeries that morning on the lawn of the Quad, and therefore I conclude that I don't need to go to the clinic after all.

Most of the defeaters in historical investigation are undercutting defeaters rather than rebutting defeaters. Typically, a historical defeater would be along the lines of a new discovery being made that shines a new light on how the culture of the time functioned and undercuts some of our earlier presuppositions, or a new way of interpreting a key text is proposed, or a gifted scholar proposes a new theory as to how to understand a complex of related issues. None of these can be tested or confirmed with anything approaching the level of certainty required for these relevant cases to be considered rebutting defeaters. Instead, most historical defeaters initially give us pause concerning our conclusions and offer a reason to reevaluate some of our beliefs. They may lead us to consider positions that we previously had not considered, or even to accept beliefs that we had previously rejected, or vice versa. Generally, when these sorts of things happen, some scholars alter their beliefs while others do not. Therefore, what qualifies as a defeater is often subjectively determined.

ABDUCTION

By now it should be obvious that historical reasoning involves a unique sort of logic, the logic of abduction.[11] Abduction is a type of pragmatic reasoning, given its formal name by Charles Sanders Peirce (1839–1914).[12] Peirce did not invent abduction; human beings have always practiced it. He did, however, give formal expression to something that people have always

---

11. For accessible and brief treatments of abduction, see the essays in Umberto Eco, "Horns, Hooves, and Insteps: Some Hypotheses on Three Types of Abduction," in *The Sign of Three: Dupin, Holmes, Peirce*, ed. Umberto Eco and Thomas A. Sebeok (Bloomington: Indiana University Press, 1988).

12. See C. S. Peirce, *Philosophical Writings of Peirce*, ed. Justus Buchler (New York: Dover, 1955), esp. 150–56, 190–217; Peirce, *Collected Papers of Charles Sanders Peirce*, ed. Charles Hartshorne, Paul Weiss, and Arthur Banks (Cambridge, MA: Harvard University Press, 1935–66), esp. V.I.VI–VII; Peirce, *Chance, Love, and Logic* (New York: Harcourt, Brace, 1923).

done, thus allowing future reasoning of this sort to be done in a more critically aware and consistent manner.

Abductive reasoning is neither deductive nor inductive. Abductive reasoning, even when done properly, doesn't lead to a *certain conclusion*, as deductive reasoning does; nor even necessarily to a *probable conclusion*, as inductive reasoning does; but rather to the *most plausible* conclusion, the likeliest explanation. One must also note that *sometimes the most plausible abductive explanation is nevertheless incorrect*: sometimes the truth is less plausible than falsehood. Furthermore, *abductive conclusions are dependent upon the available evidence*. Rarely do historians have access to all the evidence they would like to have. Therefore, abductive conclusions, including historical conclusions, must be reassessed when additional evidence becomes available. And sometimes a more plausible explanation comes from this reassessment. Abduction also allows that sometimes historians encounter situations for which they have no satisfying explanation at the moment.

Abductive reasoning is subjective because plausibility is at least to some degree in the eye of the beholder. One should note, however, that abductive reasoning is not only *subjective* but also *critical.* There are criteria or broadly agreed-upon principles by which historical reasoning is conducted. Different historians will use different criteria to assess historical explanations. Below are some of the most frequently used criteria.

— *Simplicity* (Ockham's razor). Is the explanation simpler than its rivals? Simply put, no pun intended, simpler explanations are less likely to be flawed than more complex explanations because they have fewer opportunities to fail than more complex explanations do.

— *Comprehensiveness.* Does the theory account for all the relevant data? Coherency and simplicity are much more easily attained if one disregards some of the data, but the conclusion is more likely to be flawed. Comprehensiveness serves as a guard to overemphasizing simplicity. I frequently tell my students: "Simplicity has a twin, and her name is sufficiency. It's foolish to try to make do with less when more is required." A simple explanation that addresses only a select portion of the evidence is more likely to be a *simplistic* explanation, and thus false. Furthermore, it may lead away from the best explanation by giving the historian a false sense of security. In the real world the criterion of comprehensiveness is difficult to apply because it is almost never the case that historians of antiquity have access to all the relevant evidence that was once available. Historians can only evaluate the evidence that they have, but they can evaluate all the evidence they have. For this reason, historians usually need to be satisfied with choosing a model that is more comprehensive over one that is less comprehensive. Most desirable is the simplest explanation that makes sense of all the evidence, or more of the evidence than other available explanations.

— *Fit to the data.* Does the explanation match the evidence that we have? Or must we "fix" the data to match the explanation? This is vital to the issues at hand—the explanation must fit the data, without adjusting the data to fit the explanation. Historians are frequently tempted, even if only subconsciously, to ignore or minimize evidence that appears contrary to their hypothesis. Generally, this is because they become so attached to their hypothesis that they get tunnel vision. A telltale sign of trying to fit the evidence to the explanation is that of speculation, especially stacking one speculative conclusion upon another. When speculation is compounded, plausibility is diminished.

— *Correlation.* Does the theory seem, as best we can tell, to describe how things as we experience them actually are? This goes for both our physical senses and our intuitions. A theory telling me that the physical world I experience with all five of my senses is illusory needs to have some serious evidence to accompany it, although on such a theory, it's not clear exactly how I, or anyone else, would recognize such evidence qua evidence. The same thing applies to my intuitions; a theory telling me that I am not genuinely free, or that Hitler was on moral footing equal to that of Saint Francis—such a theory will need serious support. Why do I say this? One word: perception. Perception is a time-honored means of gathering evidence about the physical and social worlds we inhabit. Sometimes the truth runs counter to our perception and intuitions, but it is generally foolish to disregard either without a good reason to do so. One warning to keep in mind is that common sense and intuition are to some degree contextual and thus vary from culture to culture. What seems obvious in twenty-first-century America may have been strongly coun-terintuitive in first-century Palestine, and vice versa. Historians should be suspicious of claims of someone being raised from the dead or virgins having babies and other such miracle claims. They should not, however, simply reject or ignore them out of hand, but rather ask: "What reason is there to believe this report?" They should demand evidence before believing such claims, but then actually examine the evidence to see if there is in fact reason to believe it. Once again, history is an a posteriori rather than an a priori discipline.

— *Coherence.* Does the theory fit with other theories that have strong support? If a theory requires that the histo-rian jettison another theory that has better evidential sup-port, or is less speculative, that should give the historian pause. The proposed theory could still be correct, but the probability of this being the case is not high. When two theories conflict, historians should reassess the evidence supporting each theory—and also the evidence and theories that support their individual premises.

Note that I mentioned evidence and *theories.* All evi-dence demands interpretation. But as I stressed earlier, one's interpretation of the evidence or opinion as to what the evidence means is not evidence! Sometimes when an interpretive theory concerning a specific item or set of data is repeated over and over, historians forget that the theory is not evidence. It may have some evidential support. It may even be correct. Nevertheless, it is still not evidence.

A case in point would be Markan priority. This is one of the most widely agreed-upon theories in New Testament studies. Yet it is a *theory*, not a *fact*. I am not arguing against Markan priority—I happen to affirm it myself—but I am pointing out that treating a theory as a fact doesn't make that theory a fact even if every scholar in the world affirms it. Truth is not determined by a vote, and a theory is not transformed into a fact by being widely affirmed. Nevertheless, when a historical hypothesis runs contrary to a theory that is more widely affirmed, alarms should go off in the mind of a historian because such opposition serves to decrease its plausibility.

— *Fruitfulness.* Does the theory answer a lingering question to which there has previously been no satisfying answer? This abductive criterion is more often relevant for scientific investigation than for history, but it also applies in history. Sometimes a historical figure behaves in a way that seems out of character, or foolish, or contrary to what someone from that culture would normally be expected to do. A hypothesis that makes sense of why that person acted in an unexpected way has more explanatory power than one that doesn't answer that question, all other things being equal.

— *Predictability.* Can predictions be based on the theory? Though this criterion is also more useful in the hard sciences than it is in historical research—because theories that make predictions can (at least in theory) be experimentally tested—it can still be applied to some degree in history.[13] This is done by the historian asking

---

13. One must distinguish between the "operational sciences," like pharmacy or chemistry, and "origins sciences," like cosmology or theoretical physics. In operational sciences the focus is upon the repeatable, whereas in origins sciences the focus is upon seeking to understand the conditions, processes, and events that led to the present state of affairs. Like history, origins science deals with events that are not repeatable and can never be repeatable. Not only can we not directly observe the big bang; we also cannot repeat it. Instead, we begin with evidence that is available to us and reason backward,

hypothetical questions as to what would probably be the result if the proposed model were correct, and then seeing if there is any historical evidence that fits with the hypothetical result.

— *Consistency.* Does the theory seem more like a conspiracy theory than something that would actually happen in real life? Does it fit within the worldview of the group being studied, or within the culture and the historical context of the time? One should be suspicious of explanations that don't seem to fit with what we know of the culture within which they are supposed to have happened.

There is no prescriptive way to apply these criteria, or even which criteria to apply, or in what order to apply them. These criteria are not like a rubric used to demonstrate to an accrediting agency that a university has been assessing their pedagogy. Neither are abductive criteria tests that a theory must pass or be rejected, like levels in a video game. Rather, they are time-tested, well-founded questions that historians use to more effectively critique historical hypotheses as to their explanatory power. They are applied ad hoc, as the situation calls for. Sometimes select criteria are used while others are not; sometimes certain criteria are deemed to be more important in context. Frequently, historians are not even aware that they are using these criteria because they have become second nature.

Abductive criteria are used to assess the overall historical hypothesis, the big-picture explanation of where all (or most) of the evidence taken together points. But historians must also assess the individual strands of the hypotheses they consider. At this point, one may fruitfully use deduction, but abduction is always in use in historical reasoning because generally the premises of a deductive argument are abductively appraised as

---

using everything we believe (or discover) about the present and the past, doing so in an effort to explain what happened (once and only once) in the past. We cannot repeat Jesus' crucifixion or resurrection (if it happened) any more than we can repeat the big bang. But we can hypothesize what would happen if X were the case, and then we can see if there is any indication that X had been the case. In many ways, history is like origins science; it is almost entirely unlike operations science.

to their truth value. The interplay of, and differences between, deduction and abduction can seem puzzling at first glance. Hopefully, explaining a few simple syllogisms will help.

1. If Professor Plum killed Miss Scarlet with the candlestick in the library in New Orleans, then Professor Plum was in New Orleans at the time of the murder.

The "If" clause of this statement, "Professor Plum killed Miss Scarlet with the candlestick in the library in New Orleans," is the "antecedent," while the "then" clause, "Professor Plum was in New Orleans at the time of the murder," is the "consequent."[14] This first premise is also the major premise of our argument.[15] If the second, or minor, premise were

2. Professor Plum killed Miss Scarlet with the candlestick in the library in New Orleans.

Then the conclusion that would logically follow would be:

3. Therefore, Professor Plum was in New Orleans at the time of the murder.

This simple syllogism is a valid argument[16] because the minor premise affirms the antecedent of the major premise and leads

---

14. The word "if" is not part of the antecedent, and the word "then" is not part of the consequent.

15. The major premise is the major premise because it contains the minor premise and the conclusion. The major premise does not have to come first in an argument, but for ease of understanding, I have stated all these arguments in their "standard form": (1) major premise, (2) minor premise, and (3) conclusion. This major premise is a conditional statement, a hypothetical statement, but it is also true because the consequent would be true if the antecedent were true. Conditional statements still have truth values: they are either true or false, because in a true conditional statement the antecedent is a *sufficient condition* to know that the consequent would necessarily follow if the antecedent were true. The consequent is a *necessary condition* for the antecedent to be true: the antecedent cannot be true without the consequent being true. Conditional statements in which the antecedent is not a sufficient condition for the consequent or the consequent is not a necessary condition for the antecedent are false.

16. A valid argument is one in which the premises completely support the argument. Validity concerns only the form, meaning the structure of an argument; validity does not guarantee the truth of any of the premises of the argument. A valid argument with all true premises is the best sort of argument, a "sound" argument. No invalid argument is sound, even if the conclusion is true, because the conclusion was reached in an improper way. Note well: the truth value of the individual premises of an argument is generally determined abductively.

with logical certainty to a true conclusion in a classical logical form known as *modus ponens* (the mode of positing).

But there is a second valid way to argue from the same major premise.

1. If Professor Plum killed Miss Scarlet with the candlestick in the library in New Orleans, then Professor Plum was in New Orleans at the time of the murder.
2. But Professor Plum was in Atlanta at the time of the murder.
3. Therefore, Professor Plum did not kill Miss Scarlet with the candlestick in the library.

This syllogism is also a valid argument because the minor premise denies the consequent of the major premise in a classical logical form known as *modus tollens* (the mode of removing).

There is a third way to argue from the same major premise.

1. If Professor Plum killed Miss Scarlet with the candlestick in the library in New Orleans, then Professor Plum was in New Orleans at the time of the murder.
2. Professor Plum was in New Orleans at the time of the murder.
3. Therefore, Professor Plum killed Miss Scarlet with the candlestick in the library.

This argument is obviously invalid and therefore unsound. The fact that Professor Plum was in New Orleans at the time of the murder is not nearly enough to prove that he killed Miss Scarlet; after all, a lot of people would have been in New Orleans at the time of the murder. This unsound argument is an example of the formal fallacy known as *affirming the consequent*.

Here's the interesting thing: *Abduction regularly affirms the consequent and is none the worse off for doing so.* Why? The short answer is that although deductive arguments are intended to *prove* that a conclusion is true, an abductive argument merely attempts to show that a conclusion is first possible, and then plausible, and thereby to persuade one that its conclusion is the likeliest explanation for the facts as they are known at that time. Significantly—and this is truly significant—when one affirms the consequent, one has avoided *modus tollens* (one has not proven that the statement is false), and therefore that statement is shown to be possibly true. Ultimately, however, the goal of an abductive argument, such as a historical hypothesis, is not to show that it is possibly true, but to demonstrate that it is the most plausible explanation for the facts as we know them to be.

This highlights once more that historians can never be 100 percent certain as to their conclusions, but they can be reasonably certain. Sometimes they can be certain beyond a reasonable doubt, or at least certain enough to believe that the conclusion is the likeliest available explanation.

CRITERIA OF AUTHENTICITY

All this talk of abduction so far has concerned how readers should assess historical hypotheses. But how do historians build hypotheses? In other words, how do historians choose which data to use in constructing their historical hypotheses?

One set of tools that historians frequently use to assess the data of research on the historical Jesus consists of the so-called criteria of authenticity. These criteria are intended to distinguish between authentic and inauthentic sayings of the historical Jesus.

On the surface, these criteria seem to flow from commonsense principles. I will briefly consider the two most frequently discussed criteria. Consider first the criterion of dissimilarity. This criterion states that if a purported saying of Jesus is not similar to the Judaism of his day and is also not similar to the theology of the early church, then it must come from the historical Jesus. If not obvious, this then seems at least like common sense: from where else could such a saying originate if not from Jesus? Many, however, have noted that our knowledge of the nature of the early church is spotty at best. What criteria will we then use to arrive at the authentic early Christian church? Furthermore, while the criterion of dissimilarity would tell us what was unique or idiosyncratic about Jesus, it would not tell us what was characteristic about him. Don't we really want to know what was characteristic of significant historical figures more than we want to know their idiosyncrasies? What if we applied this criterion to Hitler? We'd have to throw out all the elements of European culture that predated him—which would include all his anti-Semitic beliefs, and also most or all of the impacts of World War II after him. What would be left?[17] Serious critique shows that this often-appealed-to criterion of authenticity has great potential to hinder the quest for Jesus.

The criterion of multiple attestation seems to smack of common sense. The principle upon which it is based is that if there is more than one source witnessing to an event or saying, then the case for authenticity is obviously strengthened. What could be more sensible than this? But this criterion can also be abused. Who exactly determines when a source is an additional source? Many, holding to the two-source solution to the Synoptic problem, as I do, maintain that if Mark and Matthew—or Mark and Luke, or all three of them—recount the same event, then that is not two or three sources but only one because Matthew and Luke copied or adapted Mark. This may well be the case, but it also might not be. Perhaps Matthew or Luke knew of this specific event independently of Mark and simply used Mark because they *agreed with Mark* rather than because they were *informed by Mark*. After all, Luke states in his introduction that reliable information was handed on to them by eyewitnesses and that he carefully investigated everything (1:1–4); and if Matthew (as one of the Twelve) actually wrote the Gospel attributed to him, then he was an eyewitness (unlike Mark). Surely it is at least possible that Matthew and

17. Anthony Le Donne pointed this out in a Brown Bag Lunch Lecture at New Orleans Baptist Theological Seminary in spring 2014.

Luke, independently of Mark, knew about some of the things that Mark records.

When Matthew and/or Luke *appear to be* in *literary agreement* with Mark, it is certainly plausible that Matthew and/or Luke *are* in *historical agreement* with Mark. (Note well: One could not conclude that Matthew and/or Luke were in historical disagreement with Mark concerning the parts of Mark that they do not include.) Perhaps Matthew and/or Luke were informed by Mark and merely copied or adapted Mark. That could be, but it prompts the question of why they did not copy or adapt all of Mark, and why they both have unique material of their own, however scant or voluminous that material is. In other words, whatever the case may be regarding literary dependence, Matthew and Luke *chose* to reuse Mark, if they did use Mark. C. Stephen Evans voices my concern well. "That we do indeed have two authors who both attest to the events in question is a fact that is more certain than any theory about the literary dependence between the two authors. Furthermore, the fact that Mark and Luke are distinct authors is logically consistent with and therefore not undermined by any literary dependence, even if the dependence is genuine."[18] There are, of course, criteria other than dissimilarity and multiple attestation. In my view they also can be abused. These are just the two most frequently appealed to in my experience.

I am not opposed to the use of criteria in research on the historical Jesus or New Testament Christology. I am concerned about the abuse of criteria in research on the historical Jesus. We must use criteria very carefully. Furthermore, I suggest that we use them as *criteria indicating authenticity*, not as *conditions required for authenticity*. They are misused when they are employed to screen out any purported statements or actions that fail to be dissimilar, or multiply attested, or some such other subjectively applied criteria. Reginald Fuller's statement concerning dissimilarity is a prime example of what I maintain

---

18. C. Stephen Evans, *The Historical Christ and the Jesus of Faith: The Incarnational Narrative as History* (Oxford: Oxford University Press, 1996), 331.

is the wrong way to use the criteria: "As regards the sayings of Jesus, tradition-historical criticism eliminates from the authentic sayings of Jesus those which are paralleled in the Jewish tradition on the one hand (apocalyptic and Rabbinic) and those which reflect the faith, practice and situations of the post-Easter Church as we know them from outside the Gospels."[19]

I could go on listing my concerns as they relate to other criteria such as embarrassment, coherence, or several other lesser-used criteria. I am encouraged that many others are also encouraging caution while some are pleading for historical-Jesus specialists to abandon the criteria altogether.[20] The criteria are best used when they are applied in a positive manner to identify material that is highly likely to be the authentic statements or acts of Jesus, not when they are used to exclude sayings or acts of Jesus. There is nothing that prevents a historian from having doubts about the genuineness of a specific saying purported to come from Jesus, but such doubts should not arise from a crude—such as hypercritical, universal—(mis)application of these criteria.

Historical reasoning is like science in some ways, but in other ways it is like art or music.[21] The best historians sense when something is out of order, or conversely when something is significant, before others do—and even before they themselves understand why they are sensing what they do. In other words, historical reasoning involves intuition as well as inspection and methodological consistency. Simply put, reading the Bible historically is a complex endeavor. Numerous tools and methods may be used fruitfully to accomplish the task. But one must exercise good judgment in choosing which tools to

19. R. H. Fuller, *The Foundations of New Testament Christology* (London: Lutterworth, 1965), 18.

20. For a useful article-length critique, see Dale C. Allison Jr., "How to Marginalize the Criteria of Authenticity," in *The Handbook for the Study of the Historical Jesus*, ed. Tom Holmén and Stanley E. Porter (Leiden: Brill, 2010), 1:3–30. For a book-length treatment of the issues related to the criteria, see Chris Keith and Anthony Le Donne, eds., *Jesus, Criteria, and the Demise of Authenticity* (New York: T&T Clark, 2012).

21. For a very brief discussion of some ways in which history and science are similar, see my "Introduction: History, Historians, and Trusting Historical Texts," in *Can We Trust the Bible on the Historical Jesus?*, by Bart D. Ehrman, Craig A. Evans, and Robert B. Stewart (Louisville, KY: Westminster John Knox Press, 2020), 4–8.

use, as well as when and how to use them. The very same tools that can, when used properly, give historians greater assurance about the authenticity of an event can also rob them of the assurance that they rightfully would have had if they had not applied the wrong tool at the wrong time. In other words, the criteria of authenticity can clear away the fog or can further cloud the issue, depending on how and when they are used.

At the end of the day there is no silver bullet, single method, or process that will always work in all situations. In historical investigation as in life, cloneliness is not next to godliness. *Ultimately the open-mindedness, common sense, and historical sensitivity of the historian are still the most crucial components in historical investigation.*

BURDEN OF PROOF

In assessing any case, one must bear in mind the burden of proof that is operative for that particular hypothesis to be rationally accepted. One must also notice the difference between the *burden of proof* and the *standard of proof.* The burden of proof identifies who has the task of persuasion. For instance, in a criminal trial the burden of proof is upon the prosecution. In a civil trial the burden of proof is upon the plaintiff. In other words, the burden of proof is always upon the party making the positive claim. When there are competing hypotheses, the burden of proof is upon both parties.

The standard of proof is the degree to which the party with the burden of proof must succeed in persuading those assessing the argument presented. In a criminal trial the burden of proof is very high. The defendant is *presumed to be not guilty* unless the prosecution proves the charged person's guilt *beyond a reasonable doubt.* In a civil trial the burden of proof is significantly lower. The standard is a simple *preponderance of the evidence,* showing that there is a greater than 50 percent likelihood that the accusation is true. The plaintiff's legal team only needs to show that the accused is probably guilty of the charge. In a civil suit the accused can still be found guilty even if there is a reasonable doubt as to the accused's guilt so long as the likelihood that the accused is guilty is deemed to be greater than the likelihood that the accused is not.

The *standard of proof* for a historical explanation is to be more plausible than other competing explanations because almost all the time there are some wildly improbable theories that nevertheless are "possible." For instance, neither you nor I can prove beyond all doubt that we are not unknowingly trapped in a simulated reality, which intelligent machines have created to distract humankind while using our bodies as an energy source, as in the movie *The Matrix*. But none of us actually thinks that we are. Why not? Because we have no evidence that we are trapped this way. What is needed for a plausible historical hypothesis is enough of the right sort of evidence to make a rational person think not only that the explanation is possible but also that it is actually true. How much evidence are we talking about? That differs from case to case and from person to person.

CUMULATIVE-CASE ARGUMENTS

Historical arguments are generally cumulative-case arguments rather than straightforward deductive arguments. To understand the difference, compare a chain to a rope.[22] Deduction works like a chain. A set of premises proceeds step by step to a conclusion.[23] If any link (premise) is weak (false), the chain (argument) fails (is unsound). Cumulative-case arguments are not like chains: rather, they are like ropes, which have many strands. No single strand can support the argument; but taken together, the rope is strong enough to bear the weight. In fact, sometimes a few strands (claims) may break (be proven false, such as by being rebutted; or insufficiently supported, as by

22. A widespread misrepresentation of cumulative-case arguments is that they are like ten leaky buckets, one inside another. But if all the strands of argument fail, the rope fails as well. The leaky-bucket analogy misses the mark.

23. The number of premises in a deductive argument does not matter; a single premise can lead to a true conclusion.

being undercut), but the rope will still hold together, though it may be frayed. Such is often the case with cumulative-case arguments. At this point I must stress that the analogy between a cumulative-case argument and a rope is just that, an analogy, and all analogies break down at some point.

Crucially, sometimes single strands of a cumulative-case argument are necessary conditions for the argument to succeed; these strands are points upon which the argument turns, strands without which the argument fails. The point is that some strands of some cumulative-case arguments are necessary conditions, but others are not. The trick is to know which strands are necessary and which are not.

Frequently, historians are "taken" by the cumulative force of the argument and evidence, without assessing the data in a systematic manner, although they could if they chose to do so. Historical verdicts are rarely so powerful that there are no loose ends or frayed strands, but overall the evidence points to a specific conclusion in the mind of the historian.

TRUTHS TAKEN TOO FAR
THAT LEAD TO BLIND ALLEYS

Certain mistakes are seemingly repeated over and over by historians. Most of them are the result of a lack of balance in how a legitimate insight is practically applied. Entire books have been written on this subject;[24] my goal is to list only a few that I think are most significant for historical research about Jesus and the early church.

A frequent mistake is that of appealing to what "most scholars believe." Sadly, "most scholars believe" frequently seems to mean "most of the scholars that I have read believe," or "the majority of people who think like me believe," rather than being the result of a scientific polling of the guild. Even when

---

24. David Hackett Fischer, *Historians' Fallacies: Toward a Logic of Historical Thought* (New York: Harper Torchbook, 1970).

there has been a legitimate survey, *truth is not determined by a vote*, even if those voting are scholars. What matters is not how many believe a hypothesis but rather why those who believe that hypothesis believe it, how well evidenced and reasoned it is, and above all else, whether that hypothesis makes the most sense of the available data by supplying the most reasonable answers to the questions arising from the data.

Yet there is a germ of common sense behind "most scholars believe" appeals. The legitimate insight is that an expert opinion is worth more than an uninformed opinion. But because history is a public discipline, it won't do simply to appeal to the majority opinion of the guild. Even scholarly consensus needs to be justified. Those who are not scholars are well within their rights to question experts as to why they believe what they say is true. But it's foolish to ignore what the majority of experts think in any field. I am not saying that the opinions of experts don't matter; I am saying—especially in the case of history— that they don't settle the matter.

Another mistake, closely related to that above, is to believe or not believe a hypothesis depending on who affirms it. Simply put, *it doesn't matter who says it if it is true.* Nevertheless, one does need to be aware of agendas. Yet an agenda does not disprove a report. The fact that someone benefits from a belief being true doesn't necessarily make that person an unreliable witness, but it does mean that those evaluating that testimony should bear in mind the witness's motivation. Still, there are cases where one may be a better witness because of being invested in the answer. Consider the case of a wife who is suspicious about her husband's many late nights working at the office. She asks, "Is my husband faithful to me?" She will definitely benefit from a positive answer to her question. Clearly, she is not a neutral party. But she will be devoted to discovering the truth of the matter precisely because she is not neutral. Sometimes being invested in a hypothesis being true or false motivates someone to work harder to discover the truth. Unfortunately, sometimes it does just the opposite. Fear of the truth can lead to a denial of the truth, or worse, a refusal even to search for it.

Another common mistake is allowing cultural context to determine what must or must not be the case with respect to specific historical figures and how they would or would not behave. An understanding of the culture of the day is vitally important for historians. Obtaining such understanding often allows hidden meanings, both historically and hermeneutically, to be grasped, thus allowing the picture to be seen in a richer, fuller, more colorful way. But this only applies to the context: it does not apply to the specific details of a narrative; it does not dictate the precise actions that can be performed by any figures in the narrative. For instance, if Jews did not associate with Samaritans at all, then Jesus and his disciples did not go through Samaria despite what John 4:4–42 states. If all Pharisees were married, then Paul must have been married despite his protestations that he was not in 1 Corinthians 7:7–8.[25] Simply put, it is foolish to deny what is reported in texts that are well evidenced because "Jews, or Romans, or Greeks, didn't think or live that way."

Historians must constantly be on guard for the abuse of proof-texting. Yet all historians at times point to texts to prove their point, or at least to serve as examples that illustrate the point they wish to make. In fact, it would be odd if a historian could find no support for a chosen position among the sources perused. But texts can be taken out of context or twisted so that they appear, at first glance, to say what they don't mean. A text that has been misinterpreted is no friend of the truth. I frequently cringe when I read pamphlets from conservative Christians that appear to treat the Bible like a cookbook (when you feel lonely, read . . . ; when you feel afraid, read . . . ; when you've been unfairly accused, read . . . ; and so on). Whether or not we should believe a historical report is not determined by how useful it is to buttress what we already believe but, after our close evaluation, by how accurate we judge it to be on what it intends to affirm. This is especially so regarding the life of Jesus. On

---

25. It is possible that Paul was a widower rather than someone who had never married. That does not affect my point: clear statements trump a knowledge of culture.

the other hand, *not* proof-texting when a text actually supports one's point is akin to behaving as though one were ignorant of what one actually knows and for which one has good evidence.

The same thing can be said about the use of harmonization.[26] All historians at times harmonize texts that seem to be saying contrary things—especially when the texts have the same author. The key here, as in the case of proof-texting, is to harmonize passages that really do plausibly fit together in a natural and enlightening fashion. When done well, harmonization sheds light on the question under investigation; but when done poorly, as when one tries to harmonize what should not be harmonized, the question is cast into even darker gloom. Simply put, bad harmonizing, like poor proof-texting, helps nobody.[27] Similarly, not harmonizing what can be harmonized helps nobody, either.

Sometimes one must recognize that ancient texts (like modern texts) were written to a particular audience for a specific reason. They were never intended to answer all the questions that modern historians might ask of them. Furthermore, historians are nearly always faced with the fact that they never have all the information that they might desire. At the end of the day, sometimes historians may need to hope for the answer to some questions to come in the future, while understanding that some questions will remain unanswered.

A frequent example of not harmonizing something that can be harmonized, in my opinion, is that of driving a wedge between the Synoptic Gospels and John. It has become commonplace in scholarship on the historical Jesus to appeal only to the Synoptics, and especially to Mark or Q, for historical

26. By "harmonization" I am not referring to a harmony of the Gospels, a book or website that places each Gospel in its own column for ease of seeing cross-references and differences in wording and order of the four traditional Gospels. Those have their purposes. I am referring here to the attempt to explain how two passages in the Gospels, whether in different Gospels or within the same Gospel, that appear to conflict with one another can be explained so as not to conflict.

27. A prime example of harmonization gone really wrong is a book by Johnston Cheney. Johnston M. Cheney and S. A. Ellison, *The Life of Christ in Stereo: The Four Gospels Combined as One* (Portland, OR: Multnomah Press, 1984). Here is one example of Cheney's contrived explanations: he attempts to resolve the question of whether Peter denied Christ three times before the cock crowed or three times before the cock crowed twice by concluding that Peter denied Jesus six times in all, three times before the cock crowed, followed by three times before he crowed a second time.

evidence or verification. There is no doubt that John is different in style and purpose than Mark, Matthew, and Luke. Furthermore, there is no doubt that John mentions many things that the Synoptics don't, and vice versa. But does this mean that the historian must choose between them? I think not. The proper response when recognizing the differences between John and the Synoptics is to read John as a different sort of history, not to conclude that John is not historical at any point. All historical texts, including John, should be read critically, but reading critically demands that we not apply a one-size-fits-all sort of criticism to documents that we know are different. It is shortsighted to ignore what the Gospel of John purports to tell readers about the historical Jesus simply because his style of presentation is different than that found in the Synoptics.

John is getting a fresh hearing from at least some historians. Consider the John, Jesus, and History section of the Society of Biblical Literature, begun in 2002. For two decades an impressive number of renowned New Testament scholars have critically investigated the possibility that there might be more reliable historical material in John than previously believed; to date they have shared some fruit of their joint endeavor in three volumes published by the Society of Biblical Literature.[28] Their collaborative research is ongoing.[29]

Furthermore, some places in the Synoptics seem surprisingly Johannine, such as the so-called Johannine Thunderbolt, the parallels found in Matthew 11:27 and Luke 10:22, found in the hypothetical Q source. Matthew 11:27 reads: "All things have been handed over to me by my Father; and no one knows the Son except the Father, and no one knows the Father except the Son and anyone to whom the Son chooses to reveal him"

---

28. Paul Anderson, Felix Just, and Tom Thatcher have edited three impressive volumes from the Jesus, John, and History section. See Paul N. Anderson, Felix Just, and Tom Thatcher, eds., *John, Jesus, and History*, vol. 1, *Critical Appraisals of Critical Views* (Atlanta: Society of Biblical Literature, 2007); vol. 2, *Aspects of Historicity in the Fourth Gospel* (2009); and vol. 3, *Glimpses of Jesus through the Johannine Lens* (2016).

29. For more on the John, Jesus, and History group see https://johannine.org/JJH.html.

(NRSV). (Matthew 11:25–26 also seems similar to John 6:37–40, 44–46.[30])

Perhaps this separation of John from the Synoptics shows a tendency to equate a low Christology with a particular style of writing and a high Christology with another. If so, this is simplistic.[31] One can express the same truth—especially when it comes to a question of identity—in dramatically different ways. A 1953 letter of C. S. Lewis illustrates this point. A little girl named Hila wrote to Lewis about an "indefinable stirring and longing" that she had when reading *The Chronicles of Narnia*. She wanted to know what the other name was that Aslan went by in our world. Lewis replied,

> As to Aslan's other name, well I want you to guess. Has there never been anyone in *this* world who (1) Arrived at the same time as Father Christmas. (2) Said he was the son of the Great Emperor. (3) Gave himself up for someone else's fault to be jeered at and killed by wicked people. (4) Came to life again. . . . Don't you really know His name in this world?[32]

Lewis did not reply: "In the beginning was the Lion, and the Lion was with the Emperor, and the Lion was the Emperor." Instead, Lewis gave the child an answer to the riddle of Aslan's identity that was more in the style of Mark, Matthew, or Luke than that of John. But the Aslanology was every bit as high. Similarly, the Synoptic evangelists don't *tell us* that Jesus is Son of God and God incarnate: instead, they *show us* that he is.

---

30. John 6:37–40, 44–46:

> Everything that the Father gives me will come to me, and anyone who comes to me I will never drive away; [38]for I have come down from heaven, not to do my own will, but the will of him who sent me. [39]And this is the will of him who sent me, that I should lose nothing of all that he has given me, but raise it up on the last day. [40]This is indeed the will of my Father, that all who see the Son and believe in him may have eternal life; and I will raise them up on the last day. . . . [44]No one can come to me unless drawn by the Father who sent me; and I will raise that person up on the last day. [45]It is written in the prophets, "And they shall all be taught by God." Everyone who has heard and learned from the Father comes to me. [46]Not that anyone has seen the Father except the one who is from God; he has seen the Father. (NRSV)

31. If this tendency is the result of a prior theological conclusion along the lines of "this couldn't be historical because we already know that belief in Jesus' divinity came late," then it is simply a case of bias.

32. C. S. Lewis, *Letters to Children*, ed. Lyle W. Dorsett and Marjorie Lamp Mead (New York: Collier, 1985), 32.

HOW JESUS SHOWS US THAT HE
BELIEVED HE WAS DIVINE

What follows is a brief outline, drawn only from the Synoptics, of some of the reasons why I think that Jesus believed himself to be divine and the early church came to think of him as the eternal and preexistent Son of God, who was incarnated. I can't defend each point at length, nor can I explain every point in detail. On some points I will offer more explanation than on others.

Like any historical proposal, this one is open to critique. I wouldn't expect anything less. *It is a cumulative-case argument*; but it is not one where some points are necessary conditions for it to succeed. It is also a case of *a fortiori reasoning*.[33] I am confident about the overall position of this cumulative case but recognize that some may disagree with me. Also, some who agree with the overall conclusion may disagree with me at points.

The primary reason a historian should believe that Jesus was aware of his divine identity is the number and variety of ways he demonstrated an awareness that he possessed an authority equal to that of Israel's God. He acted in word and deed in ways in which only Israel's God had authority to act. These ways include the following:

— *Authority to forgive sins* (Matt. 9:1–8; Mark 2:1–12; Luke 5:17–26). Significantly, the scribes point out the implications of Jesus' claim to have authority to forgive sins: "Why does this fellow speak in this way? It is blasphemy! Who can forgive sins but God alone?" (Mark 2:7 NRSV).
— *Authority over the Sabbath* (Matt. 12:1–8; Mark 2:23–28; Luke 6:1–5).
— *Authority over the Torah* (esp. in Matt. 5:21–48, in the Sermon on the Mount). Sometimes in this section, Jesus

---

33. An a fortiori argument is a limited, more modest argument in which the conclusion is made even more certain if one grants some additional proposition. The following is an example of a fortiori reasoning: "If I am too old to play Little League Baseball, then obviously my father is too old as well." My sketch is an a fortiori argument in that I have not appealed to material from John's Gospel in this sketch. If material from John is admitted, then the case becomes even stronger.

may be correcting rabbinic interpretations of the Law, but at times—especially in Matthew 5:21–30, commandments about murder and adultery—he clearly has the written Law in view.

—*Authority over the Passover.* Jesus reshaped it in such a way that it memorialized his death and commemorated a new covenant (Matt. 26:26–29; Mark 14:22–25; Luke 22:14–23).

—*Authority over Satan and demons* (Matt. 8:16, 32; 12:28; Mark 1:23–28, 34, 39; 3:11–12, 22–30; 5:1–13; 9:25–27; Luke 4:41; 8:26–33; 11:14–20). Some of the demons even speak to Jesus and confess him as Son of God.

—*Authority to render eternal judgment, based on how individuals responded to him* (Matt. 25:31–46, parable of Judgment of the Sheep and Goats).[34]

—*Authority over nature.* Jesus' authority over nature is seen in many ways. His authority is seen in his many healings, some of which were detailed to one degree or another, many of which were simply noted as a regular part of proclaiming the kingdom of God. Included among his miracles are raising the dead (Luke 7:11–17; Mark 5:21–43, esp. 5:25–43; Luke 8:49–56), calming storms (Matt. 8:23–27; Mark 4:35–41; Luke 8:22–25), feeding multitudes from a single meal (Mark 6:30–44; 8:1–10), walking on water (Matt. 14:22–33), and cursing the fig tree (Matt. 21:18–22; Mark 11:12–14, 20–22). Significantly, Jesus doesn't generally appeal to his Father: he just performs miracles, sometimes by simply speaking a word, as God does in the Genesis creation story.

—*Authority of his own words.* Jesus' use of "Amen" is unlike any other Jewish figure in Scripture or without. In the Greek text, "Amen," a loan word from Aramaic and/or

---

34. Lest one think that Jesus is referring to another as the Son of Man in this passage, immediately afterward one reads in Matt. 26:1–2 NRSV: "When Jesus had finished saying all these things, he said to his disciples, 'You know that after two days the Passover is coming, and the Son of Man will be handed over to be crucified.'" It seems clear that Jesus uses "Son of Man" to refer to himself.

Hebrew, is used over fifty times by Jesus in the Synoptic Gospels. Many of these instances are prophetic statements, particularly about eternal rewards and one's rank at the end of the age.[35] Unlike an Old Testament prophet, he does not say, "Thus says the Lord," nor does he recite an incantation or cite a Rabbi; he simply states at the beginning that his word is true and authoritative.

—*Authority to establish the New Israel.* Jesus does this by calling twelve apostles (Matt. 10:2–4; Mark 3:14–19; Luke 6:13–16).[36]

—*Authority to equate his words with God's word.* Compare the words of Israel's God in Isaiah 40:8: "The grass withers, the flower fades; but the word of our God will stand forever," to Jesus' words in Mark 13:31: "Heaven and earth will pass away, but my words will not pass away" (NRSV).

This has been a minimalist sketch of a few of the reasons a historian can determine that Jesus believed himself to be God, which would explain why the early church after his resurrection began to proclaim that he was equal to Israel's God. If we include other New Testament books, especially the Gospel of John, then, as in any a fortiori argument, the case is strengthened even more.[37]

This is a bit of my personal thinking about the question at the heart of this book. Bart Ehrman and Michael Bird will have much more to say on this and other issues in what follows. Ehrman's book *How Jesus Became God: The Exaltation of a Jewish Preacher from Galilee*[38] is what prompted the debate

---

35. See especially Matt. 6:2, 5; 6:16; 10:15, 23, 42//Mark 9:41; Matt. 11:11; 16:28; 18:3//Mark 10:15//Luke 18:17; Matt. 18:18; 19:28; 21:31; Mark 3:28; 10:29–31//Luke 18:29–30; and Luke 23:43.

36. Significantly, Jesus is not one of the Twelve: he stands above and apart from them as God does in relation to Israel. He is the one who elects, just as YHWH elected Israel.

37. Of special significance outside of John is Phil. 2:5–11, where one not only finds both incarnation and exaltation in the same passage but also an allusion to Isa. 45:23. The late Larry Hurtado, to whom we dedicate this book, marveled: "The utterly remarkable allusion to Isaiah 45:23 in Philippians 2:10–11 involves finding a reference to Christ as *Kyrios* as well as God in what is perhaps the most stridently monotheistic passage in the Old Testament!" Larry Hurtado, *Lord Jesus Christ: Devotion to Jesus in Earliest Christianity* (Grand Rapids: Wm. B. Eerdmans Publishing Co., 2003), 73.

38. Bart D. Ehrman, *How Jesus Became God: The Exaltation of a Jewish Preacher from Galilee* (San Francisco: HarperOne, 2014).

that follows. *How Jesus Became God* is a clearly written, serious proposal. Ehrman does not simply rehearse the arguments of Harnack, Bousset, and Bultmann, although he follows them at points, especially on how the Gospels came to be as they are. In particular, he does not argue that the earliest Jewish church saw Jesus merely as a human messiah, but that at some point in the mission to Gentiles, Christianity morphed into a hellenized savior cult. Instead, he proposes that, almost immediately after Jesus' death, the earliest Christians believed that Jesus had been made divine and exalted to the right hand of God. Furthermore, he shows the sort of modesty that I've argued a historian should have by reversing his earlier published position concerning the question of whether or not Jesus was buried after his crucifixion.

Michael Bird edited a response to Ehrman's book titled *How God Became Jesus: The Real Origins of Belief in Jesus' Divine Nature—A Response to Bart Ehrman.*[39] I encourage you to read both books—after you read this one! What follows is a serious but respectful conversation on New Testament and early church Christology. I know that you will benefit from reading it regardless of what your presuppositions are at this moment or what your conclusions are after reading this book.

---

39. Michael F. Bird, *How God Became Jesus: The Real Origins of Belief in Jesus' Divine Nature—A Response to Bart Ehrman* (Grand Rapids: Zondervan Publishing House, 2014). Interestingly, both this book and Ehrman's *How Jesus Became God* were released on the same day because Harper owns Zondervan (from 1996 onward).

When Did Jesus Become God?

A Christological Debate between
Bart D. Ehrman and Michael F. Bird

BART EHRMAN: OPENING STATEMENT

Thank you very much. Hello. Thank you all for coming out. It's a pleasure being here with you. This will be my third time doing a debate with you here. I've enjoyed it each time so far. I am really glad to be able to talk with you, and I appreciate the words of the president of the institution, that you welcome other voices, because mine will indeed be a different voice from what one normally hears from this platform.

Our talks tonight are about: How did Jesus become God? Let me just ask: How many of you would agree that Jesus is God? (*Laughs.*) Right. (*Everyone laughs.*) How many of you would love to see me get creamed? (*Everyone laughs.*) Okay, good, thanks. And so it goes. Well at least I know what I am up against. So, let me start by just explaining what I see to be the terms of the question. There is a theological question you could ask, "Is Jesus God?" And almost all of you think that the answer is yes. I will not be disputing that or debating that. I am not going to be talking about whether I think Jesus was God or not, or whether you should think Jesus was God or not. That is a theological question, a question involved with belief in Jesus as a divine being. In this talk I am not interested in discussing this theological question but, instead, a historical one.

My historical question is this: "When did the followers of Jesus start believing that he was God?" And when they started to believe he was God, what did they mean by that? You might think there is only one thing you can mean. If Jesus is God, then that just means one thing, right? Wrong. Throughout Christian history, there have been numerous ways people have understood how Jesus is God. So, saying he is God is the beginning of the question, not the end of it. I am actually going to start at the end, or at least at a point closer to the end. I start with a very famous controversy that happened in the fourth Christian century, about three hundred years after Jesus, the so-called Arian controversy.

The Arian controversy rose to popular knowledge some years ago when Dan Brown wrote *The Da Vinci Code*.[40] In *The Da Vinci Code*, we learn that at the famous Council of Nicaea, in the year 325, Christians decided that Jesus would be the Son of God. They took a vote, which became a close vote, but Jesus ended up winning out, so he became the Son of God. That is in *The Da Vinci Code*. When I am teaching my students at Chapel Hill that if they want to learn about the history of the Middle Ages, the way to do that is not to watch the film *Monty Python and the Holy Grail*. And if they want to learn about the history of early Christianity, the way to do that is not by reading Dan Brown.

Let me tell you what really happened at the Council of Nicaea, with regard to the Arian Controversy. An influential Christian leader in Alexandria, Egypt, named Arius, developed his theological views in ways that he thought were perfectly orthodox, perfectly true and correct, and biblical. His view about Christ was that Christ was God. Christ was a divine being. He was the Son of God and he was God. But how could Christ be God if God was God and there not be two Gods? And

---

40. Dan Brown, *The Da Vinci Code* (New York: Doubleday, 2003).

how could God the Father be almighty and Christ be almighty? If both are almighty, then neither of them is almighty. Only one being can be almighty. And so, Arius maintained that in eternity past, God the Father alone existed, but he wasn't the Father yet. God begot a son. God, in effect, brought Christ into being as a second-level divinity, a secondary divinity. He wasn't equal to God. Nobody can be equal with God the Father. He was a secondary-level divinity. There was a time before which Christ did not exist. In other words, Christ came into being at a certain point in time, as a secondary divinity, lower than God the Father. Then Christ, through the power of the Father, created the universe, and Christ became a human being to die on the cross.

This was Arius's view. His view was popular throughout much of Christendom. The basic view had been around for a long time; yet Arius formulated it in an especially persuasive way, and after Arius's day, people continued to hold this view. His bishop in Alexandria was a man named Alexander, who took exception to Arius's view. In Alexander's view, there never was a time when Christ did not exist. Christ had always existed. He wasn't begotten by God at some point in time. He had always been begotten by God, and he wasn't a secondary divinity. He was equal with God the Father. God the Father and God the Son are completely equal in every way, and they always have been forever and ever. That was Alexander's view.

There was a big debate about this that led ultimately to the Council of Nicaea, in the year 325. A council of bishops from around the world, mainly from the eastern part of Christianity, came together to debate the issue. They ended up agreeing, not with Arius, but with Alexander. That became the standard view, which came to be incorporated in the document that is called the Nicene Creed. The Nicene Creed is still recited by people in various Christian denominations today. It was a foundational document that emerged ultimately out of this Council of Nicaea in the year 325.

This creed is especially concerned to define who Christ is. Here are some statements and emphases from the Nicene

Creed: "Jesus Christ is the only Son of God. He is eternally begotten of the Father [not just temporarily at one time, but he is eternally begotten of the Father]. He is God from God, light from light, true God from true God. He never came into being. He has always existed. He is begotten, not made. And he is of one being with the Father. God the Father and God the Son have the same essence. They are of the same substance. They are coeternal, co-powerful. They are equal in every way and always have been."

This was the view that came out of the Council of Nicaea, when Christ is confessed as fully God. So, the Council of Nicaea is not when they decided that Jesus was going to be the Son of God. Everybody at the Council of Nicaea agreed that Jesus was the Son of God. The question was *in what sense* he is the Son of God, and one side won those debates. That is the Council of Nicaea, in the year 325. Let's go back to an earlier period, to the earliest Gospel we have that talks about Jesus, to see whether it has a similar view of Jesus or not.

The earliest Gospel we have in the New Testament is the Gospel of Mark. This is not a debated point. Well, everything is debatable, but almost nobody debates this. You will not have a Greer-Heard symposium on whether Mark was the first Gospel. It was the first Gospel. What was Mark's view of Jesus? Mark has an interesting and compelling view of Jesus. Among other things, Mark certainly thinks Jesus is the Messiah, the Son of God. Mark's Gospel begins by saying that it is the Gospel of Jesus the Messiah, and throughout the Gospel, Jesus is called the Son of God. Yet it is quite interesting to observe who knows that Jesus is the Son of God in the Gospel of Mark. Now, I am not talking about what John says or what Luke says or what Matthew says. I am thinking that Mark wrote his Gospel, and if somebody read his Gospel, what would they think about Jesus? Well, they would think he was the Son of God. But who in the narrative of Mark knows that Jesus is the Son of God?

The interesting thing about Mark—again, this is common knowledge, nothing weird to me, and you will see it yourself if you just read Mark's Gospel—the strangest thing about Mark's Gospel is that nobody can figure out who Jesus is. The reader knows who he is because Mark tells you he is the Son of God (1:1). As you read the Gospel, you realize he is the Son of God, for example, by all the miracles he performs. He is the Son of God. But nobody *in the story* knows that he is the Son of God: the first eight chapters are all about people not figuring it out.

Jesus' family, in Mark 3, thinks that Jesus has gone out of his mind, and they come to take him out of the public view. In Mark 3 his family, his mother, and his brothers and sisters think that he has gone crazy. The people in his hometown can't understand how Jesus can deliver such teachings (6:2–6). "Isn't he the carpenter? His four brothers are here with us? His sisters? How does he know all of this?" They can't figure out who he is. The Jewish leaders don't know who Jesus is. They don't think he is the Son of God. They think he does miracles because he is possessed by the devil. He has Beelzebul within him (Mark 3:21–27). That's why he can cast out demons. And even Jesus' own disciples can't figure out who he is. In chapter 6, Mark tells us they did not understand (6:52). Chapter 8 of Mark, Jesus asks them, "Do you not yet understand?" No! The answer is that the disciples can't figure out who he is (8:14–21).

And then comes a key moment in Mark's Gospel, halfway through the narrative. Jesus is talking to his disciples, and he asks them, "Who do people say that I am?" And the disciples say, "Well, some say you are John the Baptist come back from the dead. Some say you are Elijah, the great prophet, or one of the other prophets." And Jesus says, "Well, who do you say that I am?" And Peter replies, "You are the Messiah" (8:27–30). Now you think, okay! Finally, eight chapters in, halfway through the Gospel, somebody's figured it out. He is the Messiah. Peter got it right. Right? Yes, kind of. Right after Peter says that, in the next verse (8:31–33), Jesus starts teaching that he, the Son of Man, must go to Jerusalem to be rejected by the scribes and elders and be executed, and that in three days he will rise from the dead. And how does Peter respond, the one who just told him he is the Messiah? Peter rebukes him: "No,

Lord, that's not going to happen to you." And Jesus says, "Get behind me, Satan, for you are thinking the things of humans, not the things of God." Peter understands that Jesus is the Messiah, but he doesn't understand what that means. He appears to think that if Jesus is the Messiah, in the sense that Jews expected a coming messiah to be, he would be a great king and warrior who drives out the enemy and sets up God's kingdom in Jerusalem, a powerful figure who would destroy the enemy. Yet Jesus is saying that the enemy will destroy *me*. Peter doesn't understand that Jesus is the suffering Messiah. Mark's Gospel is about how Jesus can be the Messiah if he suffers and dies. For Mark, Jesus must suffer and die. He is the Messiah because he is the *suffering Messiah*.

This is a long way from the controversy over Arianism. When Jesus says, "Who do people say that I am?" the disciples do not reply, "Well, some people think you are equal with the Father, have always existed, and there never was a time before which you did not exist. And well, some of us actually think that you . . . ; we think the opposite. We think, in fact, that you did come into being at some point in eternity past." That is not the issue. That is nowhere near the issue. It is not discussed in the Gospel of Mark, which deals with a completely different business. This leads to my question: How do you get from point *A* to point *B*? How do you get from Mark's understanding of Jesus as the Messiah who needs to suffer for the sins of the world, to Alexander's understanding of Jesus as a person who is coequal with God, as powerful as God, equal with God in every way, who has existed eternally from eternity past? How do you get from one to the other? Well, I have a thesis about that.

First, during Jesus' lifetime, his disciples did not believe he was God. That should not be controversial. In Mark, they can't even figure what kind of Messiah he is, let alone whether he is God or not. The issue Are you God or not? doesn't come up in the Gospel of Mark. During his lifetime, Jesus' followers didn't have any inkling that he was God. But after Jesus' lifetime, his disciples did believe he was God. There is one thing that changed their mind. *They came to believe in the resurrection.*

The resurrection is the absolute key. Why did the followers of Jesus come to believe that he had been raised from the dead?

Once again, I am simply repeating what is in the Bible itself. There are two phenomena that people often point to as evidence for why the disciples thought Jesus was raised from the dead. The first is *an empty tomb*. Three days after Jesus had died, the tomb was empty. It's stated in Matthew, Mark, Luke, and John that the tomb is empty. It is false that anybody believed because of the empty tomb. People today might be convinced that if the tomb was empty, Jesus must have been raised from the dead. But nobody in the New Testament comes to believe that Jesus was raised from the dead based on the empty tomb. Think about the Gospel of John (20:1–15). Mary goes to the tomb and finds it empty. And what does she conclude? That somebody stole his body. That's exactly what you would think if someone was buried in a tomb, and you went there three days later and found it empty: you wouldn't think resurrection. No! You'd think of grave robbers, or you'd think, "Hey, I'm at the wrong tomb!" The empty tomb isn't going to convince anybody and didn't convince anybody.

What convinced people is that Jesus appeared to people. It is the *appearance of Jesus* alive again after his death that convinced people he had been raised from the dead. Several people almost certainly claimed to see Jesus alive afterward. Historically, I think, these people really did claim that they saw Jesus alive afterward. Peter figures prominently in these narratives as one who saw Jesus. According to Paul, Peter was the first to see Jesus after his death. Paul himself says that he had a vision of Jesus. He is unambiguous about it. In the Gospels, Mary is the one who goes to the tomb and learns that he has been raised from the dead and then sees him. And so there it is: Peter, Paul, and Mary. (*Everyone laughs.*)

What did these people conclude once they came to think that Jesus was raised from the dead? Well, that is a very interesting question. Suppose we are not living in the twenty-first century, but in the first century. What do we think in the first century if we accept that a person has been exalted to heaven?

Now, when the early Christians came to believe that Jesus was raised from the dead, they didn't think it was a near-death experience, that he never really died, that it just seemed as though he died, the way we have reports of near-death experiences. They thought that if Jesus had been raised from the dead, it wasn't that his body came back to life for another twenty years. It was not that he was going to die again. He is going to live forever, they believed. He has been taken up to heaven, and he is seated at the right hand of God Almighty. What did people in ancient centuries think about somebody who, after death, had been taken up to heaven? It's quite clear what ancient peoples assumed about that, because we have numerous reports of how ancient people explained such accounts.

The Romans believed that the founder of the city of Rome, Romulus, had been taken up to heaven at his death. There is a story about it in the Roman historian Livy. This is the Romulus who had founded the city, and the city is going strong. The senate is in place. They have a functioning army. Romulus and the senators are sitting next to each other on a platform like this, and the army is marching in front of them as a parade. A thunderstorm comes up, we are told in Livy, and it grows dark. A fog comes, and when the fog lifts, Romulus isn't there anymore. He's not on his throne. What happened to him? What they said happened to him is that he was taken up to heaven, and at that point they started worshiping him as a god. He became the god Quirinus, who was one of the three main deities, one of the three main gods, for ancient Rome. This was Romulus the man, taken up to heaven, "hailed . . . as a god" (Livy, *History of Rome* 1.16).

Such beliefs happened not just in Roman circles, but also in Jewish circles. Some Jewish thinkers at the time of the New Testament thought that Moses had been taken up to heaven at his death and had become a god. We have clear evidence of this from Philo, the Jewish philosopher who taught in Alexandria, Egypt. Philo wrote several books about Moses. In one of these, he says that when Moses died, he was taken up into heaven and became a divine being: he became a godlike figure. Not just pagans but also Jews thought an exalted figure who went up to heaven when he died became a god.

Jesus' earliest followers believed he had been taken up into heaven. What were they supposed to think about that? They thought what anybody at the time would think: he had been made a divine being. And so, the earliest christological views—the earliest views of who Christ was—were that at the resurrection, God made Jesus a divine being. It was at the resurrection that Jesus became the Son of God. Again, this isn't just something that I have made up. You can find it in your Bibles. There is a speech of Paul in the book of Acts 13:32–33. This is what Paul says, "The promises God made to our ancestors he has now fulfilled to us, their children, by raising Jesus from the dead, as it is written in the second Psalm, 'You are my son; today I have begotten you'" (cf. NRSV). By raising Jesus from the dead he has fulfilled the promises because of the Scripture that says, "You are my Son; today I have begotten you." What is today? It is the day of the resurrection. That's when God made Jesus the Son of God. Or as Peter says in Acts 2:36, at his resurrection, "God made him both Lord and Messiah/Christ." The earliest followers of Jesus thought it was at the resurrection that God made Jesus into a divine being. Now again, I'm not saying that I think that you should have that view. I'm not saying you should reject that view. I'm saying this was the earliest Christian view.

This is sometimes called an *adoptionist* Christology, the idea that God adopted Jesus to be his Son. When we hear about adoption today, we sometimes don't treat or think about adopted people the way we should. We think, you know, an adopted child is not quite the same as a blood child. In the ancient world, it was the adopted child who was superior to the blood child. Julius Caesar had two sons. One of them was a son by blood, a son he had with Cleopatra. You've probably never heard of him. His name was Caesarean. Julius Caesar had a second son, who wasn't a blood son. This was his adopted son, the one he adopted to be his heir. You've probably heard of him. He was Caesar Augustus, the most powerful figure in the ancient world. The adopted son was the one who mattered. In this view of things, God adopted Christ to be his Son, which means he made him his heir. He gave him all his power, his authority, and his prestige. This is an amazing view of things, and it's the view the earliest Christians had of Jesus, that at his resurrection God had adopted him.

There is a very famous scholar of the twentieth century, a New Testament scholar, whom some of you may have known. If you are in seminary, you certainly know him: Raymond Brown, one of the great New Testament interpreters of the second half of the twentieth century. Raymond Brown had a view that I think is very persuasive, that the Christians—as they thought more and more about how Christ had been adopted to be God, how he had been exalted to a divine status—pushed the moment at which that exaltation had happened backward. They started out when they believed in the resurrection, thinking God has made Jesus his Son at the resurrection. But they thought about it for a little while longer, and they thought, you know, surely Christ was the Son of God, not just at his resurrection: he must have been the Son of God for his entire ministry. And so they started telling stories about his baptism. Jesus gets baptized. He comes up out of the water. The heavens split open. The Spirit of God descends upon him, and a voice comes from heaven. In Luke's Gospel (3:22), what does the voice say? "You are my Son; today I have begotten you." It's at the baptism. So, he was the Son of God for his entire ministry.

People started thinking about it more, and they said, you know, actually, he must have been the Son of God for his entire life, not just starting with his baptism. And so they pushed it back further, to his birth. Now in Mark's Gospel, Jesus starts at his baptism, and he hears the voice from heaven. There is no birth of Jesus reported in Mark. There is a birth of Jesus in Matthew and Luke, and it's a remarkable story, as you all know. Jesus' mother is a virgin. Why is she a virgin? Because God is his Father. Jesus becomes the Son of God already at his birth. In Luke 1, the angel Gabriel tells Mary that she is going to bear a son, and she says, "I've never known a man. How will I have a son?" And he says, "The power of the Most High will come upon you. The Holy Spirit will overshadow you. The one who is born of you will, therefore, be called the Son of God." He will be called the Son of God because, for Luke, God is literally his father. Thus Jesus was originally thought of as Son of God at his resurrection, then at his baptism, then at his birth, and then they thought more about it and pushed it back even further. Jesus must have been the Son of God from eternity past. If you read Matthew and Luke carefully, where you read about the virgin-birth story, there is no hint there that Jesus existed *before* the virgin birth. Read them carefully. In Matthew and Luke, it's not that a preexistent divine being, the Christ, had become incarnate through the Virgin Mary. In Matthew and Luke, Jesus comes into existence with the Virgin Mary, when God's Spirit makes her pregnant.

Yet as people pondered it more, they thought he must have been the Son of God from eternity past, so they started developing a *different view*, a view that is not an exaltation view, not a view where a human becomes a divine being. They started developing a view of incarnation. The word "incarnation" means something like "having come in the flesh." An incarnation view holds that Christ came into the world after existing before in the heavenly realm. Christ was a divine being who became a human being. This is not the view of Mark. It is not the view of Matthew and Luke. It is the view of the Gospel of John. In the Gospel of John, Christ is not born of a virgin. In the Gospel of John, "In the beginning was the Word, and the Word was with God, and the Word was God. He was in the beginning with God. All things came into being through him, and apart from him, nothing came into being that came into being. In him is life, and his life was the light of humans. . . . And the word became flesh and dwelt among us" [cf. 1:1–4, 14]. The word become flesh is Jesus Christ. The Gospel of John understands that Christ was a preexistent divine being who became a human being. That is an *incarnation Christology*, as opposed to the *exaltation Christology* you find in other early Christians.

Once Christians started thinking more widely, that Jesus had been a preexistent divine being, they started debating in what sense he was a divine being:

"If he was a divine being, how was he a human being? Or was he a human being?"

"If he is a divine being, and since God is a divine being, you have two divine beings; so don't you have two Gods? Or do you have only one God?"

"No, we have one God."

"Is Jesus then God?"

"Yes."

"Is God the Father also God?"

"Yes."

"So, you have two Gods?"

"No, we have one God."

And so the debates continued. Some Christians thought that in fact Christ was God because he was fully God. He was God who appeared to be a human being. God can't really be a human being any more than a human being can really be a rock. These are different things. So, a view developed called *Docetism*, which comes from a Greek word *dokeō*, meaning "to seem" or "to appear." Some Christians in the second and third Christian centuries said, "Christ was God, and he only seemed to be a human. He only appeared like a human." I need to say that most of my students probably think this. I think most of my students believe that since Christ was God, he could not really be a human being. So, he was fully omnipotent and omniscient, even as an infant. So, you know, as a two-year-old boy, Jesus could have spoken Swahili if he had wanted to, because he is God. He could do anything, right?

Well, this view lost out because Christian theologians said, "If Christ was not human, he could not die for the sins of the world. If he did not really have blood, he could not shed his blood. Salvation requires that he not only be divine, but that he also be human." So the *docetic* view lost out.

There were other Christians who wanted to say—in the second and third Christian centuries, so I'm talking one hundred or two hundred years after the Gospels, yet before Arius (250/256–336 CE)—some Christians said, "Actually, Christ is both human and divine, but it's because of this: There was a man Jesus, who was very righteous; at some point in his life, say his baptism, a divine being from heaven entered into him. Christ was a divine being who entered into the man Jesus, so that Jesus Christ is both human and divine because he has a human part and he has a divine part. So, there are two of them [united on earth]. Then when the man Jesus died, the Christ went up to heaven." I call this a *separationist* view because it separates Jesus from the Christ. That was another view that was declared a heresy, because if Jesus isn't completely human and if he isn't completely God, at one and the same time, then you are not dealing with one person but with two persons; yet Jesus Christ is one person, not two persons. God is one, and Christ is one. The church is one. There is "one Lord, one faith, one baptism" (Eph. 4:4–5). There is one, not two. This view ended up losing.

A more interesting view in some ways is what scholars have called *modalism*. For some time, this was the standard view in Christianity. Even its opponents said most people held to this view. Even the leaders of the church of Rome held to this view at the end of the second century. It's called modalism because it says that God exists in three modes—just as I myself, Bart Ehrman, am now at one and the same time the son to my father, the brother to my sister, and the father to my children. I am a son, a brother, and a father at the same time. And God is like that. God is three persons—Father, Son, and Spirit—but there is only one God. There is not three of him. I am not three different persons. I am one person. I am son, brother, father. God is three persons, Father, Son, and Holy Spirit. So this is a view called *modalism* because God exists in three modes of existence.

This view ended up losing out too, even though it was quite popular for a long time, and some people today still hold a view like this, but it ended up losing out. It ended up losing out because surely the Father and the Son are different from

one another. If you are the father of a son, you can't be the son
that you have fathered. They must be different. And you know,
when Jesus was on earth, he sometimes would pray to God the
Father. He was not just talking to himself. So this view ended
up being seen as problematic as well.

This modalist view was popular in Rome especially and was
the view of the bishops of Rome, persons later called "pope."
Eventually, then, it was turned back by people who held to
a different view, the Trinity. In the context of arguing about
modalism, one of the church fathers, a man named Tertullian
(ca. 155–ca. 220), devised the term *Trinity*. The Trinity refers
to the three persons as separate persons, individual persons,
all of whom are God. Now, I should say that Arius held to a
doctrine of the Trinity. Arius believed in God the Father, Son,
and Holy Spirit, but he thought the Son and the Holy Spirit
were inferior to God the Father, because you cannot have two
beings that are almighty. Why? If two beings are almighty, neither one of them is almighty: they *share* the might. And so
only *one* can be almighty. And by the way, that was the view of
Tertullian too, who devised the term *Trinity*. He thought the
Son was subordinate to the Father, but eventually this view
lost out.

It was superseded by the view that there is a Trinity of three
beings, all of whom are God. They are equally God. They are
equally powerful, equally all-knowledgeable, equally eternal.
They have all existed forever. There are three of them, Father,
Son, and Spirit. And yet, there is only one God. There is one
God manifest in three persons.

"But if you have three of them, there are three Gods, right?"

"No, there is only one God."

"Okay, if there is one, then there are not three, right?"

"No, there are three."

"Well, that doesn't make any sense."

"Right! If it made any sense, it wouldn't be a mystery."

The Trinity is a *mystery*, which means you cannot understand it, and if you think you understand it, you misunder-
stand it. This became the traditional view of Christianity. All

four of these views—Docetism, separationism, modalism, and the Trinity—all four of these are logical outworkings of the view that Christ is God while God is God. They have different logics that drive them, but all four of them are logical. They all make sense. It's just that one of those views ended up becoming the orthodox view, that there are three persons, all of whom are God, and there is only one God.

My point is that the earliest Christians did not think this. You will not find this doctrine in the New Testament. The Trinity is a later doctrine that developed out of earlier views. The earliest Christians came to believe that Jesus had been exalted to God's right hand at his resurrection. And they thought that, therefore, God had made him a divine being. Three hundred years later, they were saying that Jesus had always existed, that he was coeternal with the Father. He was co-omniscient with the Father. And that he, in fact, was God Almighty himself, the Creator of all things.

MICHAEL BIRD: OPENING STATEMENT

G'day! Yes, I will use my charming Aussie accent to win over my audience. Out of curiosity, who wants to see me get creamed? Anyone? Yes, we do have some—and Bart as well! What? But I thought all you Americans love Australians? We invented *Crocodile Dundee* and the Outback Steakhouse. Without us, there is no Outback Bowl.

The theme of this forum is "When Did Jesus Become God?" This pertains to mapping the origins of belief in Jesus' divinity. There are several topics that we could cover. We could discuss what Jesus thought about himself. We could talk about the evangelists, the apostle Paul, post-70 developments, the second and third centuries, and so forth. But let me tell you what I am not going to argue: I am not going to argue that Jesus more or less cruised around, saying, "Hi, I'm God, second person of the Trinity. Soon I am going to die for your sins, and then I'd like for all of you to worship me." I'm not going to argue anything like that. I will not argue that the early church basically down-loaded the Nicene Theology app ten seconds after the resurrec-tion. There was diversity in the early church. A development of theology definitely took place, as if something momentous had happened, and the next four hundred years were based around asking, "Who the heck was that guy?" That is largely what was driving theology.

Instead, of all of the topics that have been discussed, there is one I want to examine with a close inspection. You see, a com-mon line in scholarship has been that the earliest view of Jesus in circulation was that Jesus was a man adopted either at his resurrection or at his baptism, where he then became the Son of God. Bart has thankfully already touched upon this. This is called *adoptionist* Christology. In adoptionism, there was a time when Jesus was not the Son of God. Divine sonship is not something that Jesus possessed for all time but something he acquired in the course of his life [or at his resurrection]. Adop-tionism is thought to be the first Christology, yet that is not the end of it. Because we know that views of Jesus eventually changed and evolved into a belief about the incarnation, that Jesus was the God of Israel made flesh, and that meant that the earlier adoptionism could be relegated to the status of a heresy.

Even though adoptionism was relegated to a kind of hereti-cal status, it did not die out. It was propagated by groups like the Ebionites, a Jewish Christian sect; holding this view were also Theodotus, a lay Christian cobbler in Rome at the end of the second century; and Paul of Samosata, a bishop of Antioch in the third century. We know—for example, as James Dunn says—that the Ebionites [2nd to 5th centuries in Palestine and Syria], the Jewish Christian group, held to an adoptionist Christology; Dunn contends that this heretical Jewish Chris-tianity would appear to be not very different from the faith of the first Jewish believers.[41]

---

41. James D. G. Dunn, *Unity and Diversity in the New Testament: An Inquiry into the Character of Earliest Christianity*, 3rd ed. (London: SCM, 2006), 242; Dunn, *Christology in the Making: A New Tes-tament Inquiry into the Origins of the Doctrine of the Incarnation*, 2nd ed. (London: SCM, 1986), 33–36.

Now, Bart has argued fairly similarly to that, suggesting that if we were to get one of the followers of Jesus to write a Gospel of Jesus within a year of his resurrection, we would find an exaltation Christology, not one of incarnation or preexistence. It would be a Christology where Jesus became the Son of God when God worked his greatest miracle on him, raising him from the dead and adopting him as his Son by exalting him to his right hand and bestowing upon him his very own power, prestige, and status. So, that's the sum of Bart's position. That would mean, rather than "in the beginning was the Word, and the Word was with God" (John 1:1), you would get something like "In the beginning was a mere man who was adopted as God's Son at the resurrection."

Now, my response to that thesis, to quote George Gershwin, is "It ain't necessarily so." I cannot prove that an adoptionist Christology did not exist among any of his followers in the middle decades of the first century, or in the early decades after the resurrection. I cannot prove that. What I think I can show is that the standard texts and the normal groups to which is attributed an adoptionist Christology do not in fact say that, or did not in fact hold that.[42]

So, what I'm going to do is look at some of these texts and discuss several of these groups: I will try to show that they did *not* exhibit adoptionist Christologies. So, let's start off with the first one. In *Romans 1:3–4*, Paul is writing to the church in Rome, and at the head of this letter, he writes about the gospel "concerning his Son, who was descended from David according to the flesh and was declared to be the Son of God in power according to the Spirit of holiness by his resurrection from the dead, Jesus Christ our Lord" (ESV). Now, Romans 1:3–4 is probably a short creedal formula that was recited in the early church and was in circulation; Paul was most likely using it because it was known to him and to his Roman audience, so he

---

42. I lay the case out more fully and thoroughly in Michael F. Bird, *Jesus the Eternal Son: Answering Adoptionist Christology* (Grand Rapids: Wm. B. Eerdmans Publishing Co., 2017).

cites or paraphrases it, to show that they're both singing off the same sheet of gospel music.

Now, what Bart—and he's not alone in this—says about this text is that from this creed, one can see that Jesus is not just the human Messiah. He is not simply the Son of God Almighty. He is both things in two phases. First, he is the Davidic Messiah, predicted in Scripture. And second, he is the exalted, divine Son. So, Jesus goes from being the human Messiah [in his earthly ministry]: with resurrection, he becomes the divine Son of God.[43] Now, Paul may have wanted to embellish that further, because it did not fit with his own view, which included preexistence. Yet, to the original framers of this creed, Jesus was the Messiah from the house of David, during his earthly life. At the resurrection, he was made something more than that. The resurrection, then, was Jesus' exaltation to divinity. I think there are three problems with this view.

Number one. I don't think resurrection necessarily makes one a divine son of God. For a start, "son of God" in the Jewish world does not usually mean a human person who has lived a meritorious life and received divine sonship after a bodily resurrection. We do know of figures who were exalted to heaven, who were taken up, figures like Enoch and Elijah. They were thought to be assumed into heaven, but they were not thereafter called a "son of God." Think of other examples; Lazarus was raised from the dead (John 11), but that did not make him a son of God. The two witnesses in the book of Revelation come back to life, but they are not treated as sons of God (Rev. 11). You do find these exalted figures, like Moses and others, treated with divine titles, so there always seems to be a certain degree of divine honor given to them, but not in the absolute sense that is normally attributed to Yahweh.

I find it interesting that scholars frequently want to find a parallel between Jesus being made divine in his resurrection and the imperial cult. You know the idea that when a Roman

43. Bart D. Ehrman, *How Jesus Became God: The Exaltation of a Jewish Preacher from Galilee* (New York: Harper One, 2014), 221.

emperor dies, he becomes a god, that sort of a thing. What I find interesting is that when a Roman emperor dies, he never becomes *a son* of a god. He becomes the "deified one": he becomes a *deus*. It is the guy left behind—the heir, who is still very much alive—who becomes "the son of god." As the adopted son still on earth, he is the one who now can have this title, son of the divine Augustus. Roman emperors do not die and thus become sons of god. The heirs who are left behind become sons of god.

Number two. The other thing we need to remember is that the titles "son of David" and "son of God" were both designations for Israel's messiah. That is rooted in the Old Testament, where we find the promise that one of David's descendants will be God's own son. That is in 2 Samuel 7. We see Israel's king ritually celebrated as the divine son, in places such as Psalms 2 and 72. There's a similar phenomenon in Jewish intertestamental literature, which looks forward to a coming son of David, the Messiah, often called the son of God, as in the Psalms of Solomon (17.21) and in the Dead Sea Scrolls (4Q252 II 1; 4Q174 I 1.10–13); also, son of David and Son of God are frequently put together in the New Testament. So, if the son of David, the Messiah, is a son of God, then we cannot say that divine sonship begins at a later point like resurrection. That's because in the creed we're examining, Jesus already is the Son of God, because he is the descendant of David. He is the messianic Son. That is what makes him the Son of God. So, there is a change in status, not from mere human to Son of God, but from being a *Davidic* son of God to being an *exalted* Son of God, a Son of God in *power* and *majesty* and that sort of thing.

Number three. In order to read this text as adoptionist, one needs to assume that Paul himself added the phrase "in power" to this creed, in order to mitigate its adoptionist content. Bart's underlying assumption is that the creed in its current [Nicene] form is not adoptionist, but before that it was. So, you had a creed that was adoptionist; then to mitigate that, to cleanse it of this adoptionist trait, Paul has added the phrase "in power," which completely changes the sense, so it is no longer adoptionist. In other words, Paul took over an adoptionist text and made it non-adoptionist.

Now, while I think Paul is working with some traditional materials he has inherited, we don't know what he added, what he expanded, what he abbreviated. When we simply do not know and yet assume that Paul must have added this phrase, to make it more palatable to his own theology, and thus that he has transformed an adoptionist creed into something non-adoptionist, that is a rather thin branch upon which to hoist a heavy argument. I rather like what Simon Gathercole says in our book: if you base your argument on a conjecture—such as assuming that "in power" was added—then your whole argument really becomes a conjecture.[44] So, like a good many other scholars, I do not see any real proof that Paul added the phrase "in power," turning this adoptionist creed into a non-adoptionist one.

To sum that bit up, being raised to life does not make you the Son of God. Yes, it could make you immortal. It could make you heavenly. You could be equal to the angels. You could recline in the bosom of Abraham. But it doesn't make you a son of God. The creed does envisage a two-stage movement, but that movement is not from being a human messiah to the Son of God in power. It is a movement from being the Davidic son of God to being the Son of God in power and majesty and the like. If the adoptionist reading is to work, it requires that the phrase "in power" be an addition, and there is no evidence for that beyond the mere assertion itself.

Let's look at our second text. This is from the *Gospel of Mark*. I think Bart touched upon this. Mark says, "In those days Jesus came from Nazareth of Galilee and was baptized by John in the Jordan. And when he came up out of the water, immediately he saw the heavens being torn open and the Spirit descending on him like a dove. And a voice came from heaven, 'You are my beloved Son; with you I am well pleased'" (1:9–11 ESV).

44. Simon Gathercole, "What Did the First Christians Think about Jesus?," in *How God Became Jesus: The Real Origins of Belief in Jesus' Divine Nature—A Response to Bart Ehrman*, ed. Michael Bird (Grand Rapids: Zondervan Publishing House, 2014), 106.

As Bart wonderfully pointed out, the Gospel of Mark is often regarded as something of an innovation in the chronology of when and how Jesus became the Son of God. As Bart explained, there was a tendency in the tradition to project Jesus' sonship earlier and earlier, and Mark represents the phase where it is being projected from the resurrection back to his baptism. Scholars place Mark within this evolving process, where divine sonship is gradually being put earlier and earlier. The Gospel of Mark, so it goes, has no Christology of preexistence: so Jesus, then, would become the Son of God at his baptism. Thus Jesus would be divine in the sense that he is adopted to be God's Son at his baptism, not [delayed till] the resurrection.

Now let me add something on this. If you are a Roman reader, and you are reading the Gospel of Mark for the first time, I certainly think it is possible that you could take it in that sense. Why? If you know about the deifications in Rome of Julius Caesar, Augustus, Claudius, and the like, you could think—and this is where divine adoption was practiced in Rome—I think someone, in their own fashion, in light of their own experiences, could take it that way. I just don't think Mark intends us to take it that way.

First, Jesus' adoption is not regarded as the reward for his virtuous life. That was largely what was argued by a number of authors in the second century, that Jesus was a virtuous man who earned, warranted, or merited divine adoption or exaltation, or something like that. If that is what Mark intended, you would expect Mark, like those later exaltationists, to articulate something similar. I think Mark is not presenting the baptism as the beginning of Jesus' story; there was a backstory. Rather, he sees it as the beginning of the gospel. So, the baptism story is not the beginning of Jesus: it is the beginning of the gospel [good news] about Jesus.

Second, the other thing we need to remember is that there are other points in the Gospel of Mark where Jesus is called a divine Son by another voice, especially at the transfiguration scene in Mark 9 and at the crucifixion scene in Mark 15. Mark envisages three christologically decisive moments

in Jesus' career, and no one of them is singularly determinative for Jesus' sonship. If a voice pronouncing Jesus as a son
implies adoption, it would mean that Jesus is adopted three
times. Once at his baptism (1:11), again at the transfiguration
(9:7), and again at the crucifixion scene. In fact, if I wanted
to have an adoptionist reading of Mark, I would be more
inclined to say he gets adopted at the crucifixion, because
that is where he dies; then he could experience some kind
of *apotheosis*, or deification. And it is a Roman soldier who
announces him to be "a son of God" (15:39 ESV note). If you
wanted to have an adoption scene in Mark, I think it would
be more likely, more logical, to have that at the crucifixion
scene rather than at the baptism. I think Mark treats that baptism, the transfiguration, and the crucifixion not as *moments
of adoption* but divine *moments of revelation*, as clarifications
as to who Jesus is.

Third, Mark's overall Christology creates a certain tension.
On the one hand, Jesus is fully and authentically human. In the
Gospel of Mark, Jesus is a good monotheist. He proclaims the
kingdom of God (1:15). He prays to God (1:35). He says, "No
one is good except God alone" (10:18 ESV). And yet, there are
other passages and actions that make it look as though Jesus is
somehow paradoxically, ambiguously to be identified with the
Lord, with the *Kyrios*.

I do think Mark does intimate Jesus' preexistence; hopefully,
Simon Gathercole will have more to say on that tomorrow.
(Gathercole shakes head no.) No? Well, read his book.[45] It's a
crackin' good read. I am thinking of how Jesus seems to belong
to the heavenly council. He transcends the heaven-and-earth
divide. The demons seem to know who he is. I think that is
implied. What I can say a bit more confidently is that in the
Gospel of Mark, use of the term for Israel's "Lord" is split,
some places meaning God, some places meaning Jesus. And it
is that way from the very beginning of the Gospel.

---

45. Simon J. Gathercole, *The Preexistent Son: Recovering the Christologies of Matthew, Mark, and Luke*
(Grand Rapids: Wm. B. Eerdmans Publishing Co., 2006).

The opening of the Gospel has John [the Baptist] preparing the way for the Lord, the coming Lord, and the one who comes is none other than . . . Jesus. Similarly, when Jesus debates with the scribes as to whether the Messiah is the son of David, Jesus quotes Psalm 110:1 to them, to the effect that the Messiah will be more than an earthly son of David, one who has his throne established by Yahweh. Similarly, at the trial scene, when he is asked if he is "the Son of the Blessed One" by Caiaphas (14:61 NRSV), Jesus responds with a combination of Daniel 7:13 and Psalm 110:1, to the effect that he will share in the lordship of Israel's God. The net effect of sharing Yahweh's throne is that Jesus stands in a relationship of "near equality with God," to use the language of Joel Marcus.[46] The inference would seem to be that Jesus is not just the son of David but also the Son of God, understood as Yahweh's co-regent. We could surmise that the exclusive divinity of the God of Israel is maintained throughout Mark. More than any other evangelist, Mark emphasized that there is one God. He stresses that more than any other of the authors. And yet, that does not seem to be done at the exclusion of Jesus. Suppose we ask, Who is the Lord in the Gospel of Mark? The paradoxical answer is "God and Jesus."

So we can sum up this point. If Mark intended to portray Jesus' baptism as an adoption, you might expect a bit more mention of his meritorious life that would warrant it, as you find in other adoptionist or exaltation authors. If a voice that calls Jesus "Son" implies his adoption, then that means that Jesus is adopted an astounding three times. Third, I don't think Mark's Christology as a whole gels with an adoptionist Christology since Jesus seems to participate in the lordship of Israel's God. In fact, I love the way Eugene Boring, a Markan specialist, puts it: "It is un-Markan to claim that Mark presents us with a human being Jesus who in the course of time is promoted to a higher ontological level, whether this can be

---

46. Joel Marcus, *Mark 8–16: A New Translation with Introduction and Commentary*, Anchor Yale Bible (New Haven: Yale University Press, 2007), 850–51.

conceived as happening at his baptism or at his resurrection/exaltation."[47]

There was a group called the *Ebionites*, whose origin and texts and a lot about them is shrouded in mystery: everything about their group is vague. Some have thought the name came from a chap named Ebion, but no one is really convinced that there was a guy by that name. [The name "Ebionites" is derived from the Hebrew word for "the poor."] Notwithstanding such caveats, many scholars remain fairly confident that this group held adoptionist beliefs, the idea that Jesus was a remarkable man chosen by God to be his Son and adopted at baptism. Now I don't think that statement is entirely false. I certainly don't think it's the best way to describe the Ebionites, either. And one of the things I find striking is that, generally speaking, Jewish authors were allergic to the idea of humans being deified. While Josephus and Philo were two Jewish authors immersed in the Hellenistic world, who did their best to negotiate their way through it and affirm as much Greek philosophy and Hellenistic culture as they could, both of them seemed to have drawn a line at the idea of worshiping a deified figure. Josephus said that God has vetoed Israel from doing it (*Against Apion* 2.76). Philo said deification was useful neither to God nor man (*On the Embassy to Gaius* 93–118, 278). Also, adoption was generally not practiced in Judea and not normally used as a way of extending one's dynasty. If an adoptionist Christology was going to emerge, it probably was not going to be on Palestinian soil, nor in the Transjordan, nor among Jewish groups, but some place where deification was practiced and adoption was also widely utilized as a way of extending one's family. I think it is more likely to be in Rome than in Palestine.

Another thing we can note: if we go through all the comments of patristic authors, they say some odd things about the Ebionites; but some of them point out that the Ebionites did

---

47. M. Eugene Boring, "Markan Christology: God-Language for Jesus?," *New Testament Studies* 45 (1999): 471.

not think that Jesus was the Son of God in any sense. That is certainly the testimony of Tertullian (*The Flesh of Christ* 14).

The one patristic author who seems to attribute views to them that are adoptionist is the author Epiphanius in the fifth century (*Refutation of All Heresies* 30.18.6). He certainly does talk about them as ones who believe that Jesus was elevated or promoted to divine status. But even then, he does not use the language of adoption. He does not describe their views with the normal Son-of-God discourse, about Jesus' unique filial relationship to God, or about his messianic office. The other thing we need to remember is that Epiphanius is also one of our unreliable authors about the Ebionites. He says several things suggesting that he is just taking information from other sources and projecting it onto the Ebionites. There is a Gospel of the Ebionites, which presents a harmonized account of Jesus' baptism, but again it is known only from Epiphanius, and we can't be really sure it was composed by the Ebionites. It was most likely composed in Greek, not in Aramaic. And, yes, there is a moment in the scene of Jesus' baptism where you hear this divine voice from heaven saying, "You are my Son," but in contrast to a lot of the evangelists, this provides a full quotation of Psalm 2:7 (Gospel of the Ebionites 4). The voice from heaven does not simply say, "You are my Son"; it says in full, "You are my Son; today I have begotten you." Many have taken that as an indication, by quoting Psalm 2:7 more fully, that the Ebionites must have had an adoptionist Christology, believing that at the moment of baptism, Jesus was begotten as the Son of God. The problem I have with that view is that Justin Martyr, when he narrates the baptism story of Jesus, also quotes Psalm 2:7, not the short form, but the longer form. "You are my Son; today I have begotten you" (Justin, *Dialogue with Trypho* 88, 103). But no one supposes that Justin Martyr was an adoptionist.

If there is one belief that the church fathers seemed to be fairly unanimous in attributing to the Ebionites, it is not that of adoptionism, but more along the lines of what Bart called a separation Christology, where an angel or the heavenly Christ descends upon Jesus at his baptism. So there was a group called the Ebionites, but I think they more likely held to a separation Christology than to an adoptionist one.

That brings us to the last group, the *Theodotians*. Theodotus of Byzantium was a leather worker or cobbler who came to Rome in the late second century, and he developed a bit of a following. You know, not bad for a leather worker to have one's own school of theology. According to Theodotus, Jesus was a mere man who was supremely virtuous. Thereafter the Spirit or Christ descended upon him at baptism, enabling him to perform miracles. Hippolytus of Rome, a contemporary of Theodotus, reports diversity among the Theodotians. Some did not think that Jesus was divine in any sense. Others believed that he was made divine at his resurrection (Hippolytus, *Refutation of All Heresies* 7.35–36). And this is where I think Bart and I would be in broad agreement. Going on the sources we have, even Theodotus cannot properly be called an adoptionist. Theodotus believed that Jesus was a mere man who received Christ or the Spirit at his baptism, and according to sources earlier than Hippolytus, he never claimed that Jesus was divine or became divine in any sense. He saw Jesus exclusively as a spirit-empowered prophet, and on this point we know nothing more. But among the Theodotians, there were other views, a mixture of beliefs about Jesus as a mere man, a separation Christology, some really strange cray-cray [crazy] speculations about Melchizedek as well. One group of the Theodotians believed that Jesus was deified after his resurrection. Those, I submit, are the first clear, authentic, full-monty [total], bona fide adoptionists, as far as the evidence goes. And that settles how and when Jesus was first adopted by God.

Coming toward a conclusion, I do not think adoptionism is expressed in a text like Romans 1:3–4, nor in the baptismal scene in the Gospel of Mark. It was not really apparent among the Ebionites: some loose connotations may be there, but it was not their main show. Theodotus did not express it; in only one chapter of the Theodotians do we find this adoptionist Christology. What that means is that the *first and earliest Christology was not adoptionist*, as far as these sources tell us.

When I discuss ancient heresies or minor christological beliefs with my students, I often tell them that sometimes the road less traveled is less traveled for a good reason. There might be some theological reasons why adoptionism was rejected as an inadequate account of Jesus. Because, besides the matter of perhaps the general incongruity with the witness of the New Testament as a whole, there's a theological reason why adoptionism was rejected. That is because adoptionism inevitably includes the belief that one can be self-justified before God, and it is at odds with the gospel of grace as the early church knew it.

Justo González argues that modern adoptionism denies the embodiment and the efficacy of grace in Jesus Christ, in favor of the view that Jesus merited divine favor by his good works. Jesus becomes the paragon, the example of the good man who is rewarded with divine honors. Viewed this way, adoptionism becomes the counterpart to the American myth that everybody can make it on their own steam, on the sweat of their own hard labor. Everyone has a chance to get to the top. But González writes, and he has in mind here largely the Hispanic church, "Jesus Christ must be more than first among the redeemed, more than local boy who makes good. He must also be the redeemer, the power from outside who breaks into our closed reality and breaks its structures of oppression. He must be more than the adopted son of God. He must be God adopting us as sons and daughters."[48] And there, my good friends, ends the lesson. Thank you very much.

BART EHRMAN: RESPONSE

Thank you, Michael. That was very lively, very interesting. Thank you very much. So, I think that was a very learned presentation, and I think Michael has ratcheted up the discussion to a higher scholarly level. I'm not sure how much I want to

---

48. Justo L. González, *Mañana: Christian Theology from a Hispanic Perspective* (Nashville: Abingdon Press, 1990), 144–45.

take him on point by point, because I only have nine minutes and thirty seconds, and interpretations of these passages are rather complicated.

His overall point is that the earliest Christians were not adoptionists. You do not have that until the Theodotians in the second century. I fundamentally disagree with him on that. Michael has sketched a highly unusual view. I have never heard anybody maintain that before, but it needs to be taken seriously. I think it overlooks key evidence. He doesn't mention, for example, these early fragments we have in the book of Acts. In 13:30–37, Paul explicitly says that what God promised to the fathers, he has now provided to us their children, by raising Jesus from the dead in fulfillment of Psalm 2:7, "You are my Son; today I have begotten you" (ESV). Or as Peter says in Acts 2:36, that by raising Jesus from the dead, "God has made him both Lord and Christ."

He does look to Romans 1:3–4, and we fundamentally disagree about several things on that passage; there Paul says that Christ was the son of David according to the flesh, but at his resurrection he was appointed to be Son of God. He was appointed to be Son of God at his resurrection. God appointed him to be Son of God by raising him from the dead. That certainly sounds like adoption, whether you have the words "in power" there or not. Now Michael says that it cannot really be referring to somebody becoming the Son of God, because in the Greco-Roman world, whoever [such as an emperor] was adopted by God [was deified and] did not become the son. I'm not quite sure I understand the logic of that. If you are adopted by somebody, you become their son. That's what adoption is.

Also, it doesn't work to say that someone raised from the dead doesn't become the son of God because Lazarus was raised from the dead, and he wasn't the son of God. Or the two figures from Revelation 11, who are not thought of as sons of God. The difference is, when Lazarus is raised from the dead, the idea is that he is going to die again. He is not raised up to heaven, and so he is not made the son of God. He is resuscitated. He is brought back to life for a while. Jesus is raised from the dead, never to die again. That's why he's made the Son of God. He's made a divine being, an immortal being, a being who won't die. I don't think it's right to say that Jesus was already the Son of God because he was descended from David. Probably every Jew on the planet today, ultimately, is descended from David. Just look at how genealogies work. And so, Jesus was not the only human being on the earth who was descended from David. So, does he want to say that everyone is the son of God? That would be fine with me, but I don't think that's really what Michael wants to argue.

Paul makes a point that in terms of his earthly life, Jesus was the son of David, thereby the Messiah. But in terms of his heavenly life, he became the Son of God at the resurrection. Just read Romans 1:3–4 for yourself. What about Mark 1:11? So, this is where the voice from heaven at the baptism says, "You are my Son, the Beloved; with you I am well pleased" (NRSV). And Michael wants to say that this cannot be God adopting Jesus to be the Son, because then he is adopted three times in Mark's Gospel, at the baptism, at the transfiguration, and at the crucifixion, because on all three occasions and in relation to Jesus, a voice says, "Son/son of God." It is an interesting point, but I think it overlooks something very important: at the baptism, the voice speaks in the second person to Jesus, in Mark's Gospel. In the text in Mark's Gospel at the baptism, the voice says, "*You* are my Son, . . . in whom I am well pleased" (1:11). That is the adoption formula when he becomes the Son of God. The voice at the transfiguration does not say, "You are my son." It does not adopt Jesus. It announces to the three disciples, "*This* is my son" (9:7). In other words, Mark is identifying that this is the one who *has become* the Son of God, and so too at the crucifixion. The Roman centurion who crucified him says, "Truly this man was the son of God" (15:39). He is acknowledging that he is a son of God. He is not making him the son of God.

It is a little unusual to argue that the Ebionites were not adoptionists. Whether they were or not doesn't matter for my case at all. It's true that some church fathers said that they had what I call a separationist Christology. Our earliest full representation of the Ebionites is actually from an author named Irenaeus, in the late second century. Irenaeus and other church fathers who talk about the Ebionites call them adoptionists. Now maybe Irenaeus didn't know what he was talking about, but he is our first heresy writer from early Christianity who gives a [rather] full list of a lot of different heresies and describes them. So, maybe they were not adoptionists. I don't know.

But I would absolutely not say that Jews were allergic to deification. That simply is not true. In my book *How Jesus Became God*, I have a thirty-seven-page chapter, example after example after example, of Jews calling beings "God," various beings other than God Almighty.[49] Moses is called "God" by Philo. Philo is not allergic to deification. Philo not only thought Moses was God; he also thought the Logos, the Word of God, was God. He calls the Logos the second God, [thus naming] two Gods. This is a Jewish author. You have this view that other beings can be gods in Scripture itself. In Psalm 45:6, God is speaking to the king of Israel. As Michael admits, this is God speaking to the king of Israel, and he says, "Your throne, O God, is forever and ever" (ESV). That's God speaking to the king: "Your throne, O God, is forever and ever." Of course, Solomon was supposed to be the son of God, as declared in 2 Samuel 7:11–14, "I will be a father to him, and he shall be a son to me" (NRSV). The kings of Israel were understood to be sons of God. Psalm 110, "The LORD says to my Lord, sit at my right hand until I make your enemies a footstool for your feet." Jews were not allergic at all to deification.

There was an early Jewish heresy that Michael actually mentioned, one studied by an important American scholar, a scholar of Judaism named Alan Segal, called "The Two Powers in Heaven" heresy, a heresy attacked by rabbis in early rabbinic literature. It was called "Two Powers in Heaven" because it maintained that somebody was sitting next to God on his throne. There was another enthroned figure next to God, who was understood in Jewish circles to be a divine being. Christians ended up saying that Jesus is that one sitting next to God. They were not coming up with something that no Jew had ever heard of. As Alan Segal himself points out, this was a view that had been around for a long time, a view that many rabbis were uncomfortable with, just as later Jews continued to be uncomfortable with the claim that Jesus was God.

So, at the end of the day, I'm not sure what Michael thinks about the question that we're talking about. We are dealing with the question How is it that Jesus came to be thought of as God? How did it happen? My view is the one that I laid out. I think that the early Christians did not think of Jesus as God during his lifetime. The evidence is rather clear about that from the earliest Gospels, Matthew, Mark, and Luke. Nobody calls him God in Matthew, Mark, and Luke. They did not think that. Well, if they did not think it, then when did they start to think it? At the resurrection. The resurrection was what made people start thinking that Jesus was God. And once they started thinking that Jesus was God, they started working out the implications. And as they thought more and more about it, their theology developed more and more until you get to the Council of Nicaea. So, I don't know what Michael's alternative to that is. But maybe at some point, he'll be able to tell us. Thank you very much.

MICHAEL BIRD: RESPONSE

Well, thank you very much, Bart. That was a great lecture: it shows some of the issues that are involved when you talk about the early church's beliefs about Jesus, how there was debate. There was genuine development in what happened, and there was a story being told here of people struggling to find the grammar, the language, and the frameworks to express who Jesus is. And it seems very clear to me, and I am sure it is to Bart, that it wasn't all worked out in the first few seconds. Nonetheless, despite Bart's precise narration of that story, there are a few points I really would like to tweak a bit. Let's go to his reading of the Gospel of Mark, and here I think Bart is correct. The Gospel of Mark is largely an apology for a *crucified* Messiah. That's the main purpose of Mark. Mark is dealing with the question "How can Jesus be the Messiah if he was crucified?" Mark is arguing that he is not the Messiah *despite* the cross, but precisely *because of* the cross. Because that's where we see him undertaking his messianic vocation. There we see him combining in himself the roles of the Suffering Servant, the kingship language we find in the Psalms, various views of the Messiah, and that kind of thing.

However, one thing that emerges in the Gospel of Mark is that Jesus is not merely a human Messiah. I don't think he is even a figure who is being made divine or is being adopted to divine sonship at his baptism. Later I will explain more of that in my talk. But for now, what I want to say is this: I think there might be a little more going in Mark's Gospel than that. For example—you pointed it out, Bart—in the first half of Mark's Gospel, nobody knows who he is. But there are some beings who *do* know who he is. The demons know who he is. When Jesus rocks up [turns up], they say, "[We] know who you are— the Holy One of God" (1:24 ESV). But a question that I have in my mind is this, and hopefully Simon will answer it: *How* do they know that? Is there kind of a demonic version of Twitter? "Watch out for the crazy Galilean guy with the beard. He is whupping our butts something fierce." How do they know who he is? How do they know he's come to destroy them?

And certainly, when we get to the end of Mark's Gospel, at the trial scene, there is this incredible moment where Caiaphas finally asks Jesus who he is: "Are you the Son of the Blessed One, or what?" (cf. Mark 14:61). And Jesus responds in language that combines Daniel 7:13 and Psalm 110:1, two texts with one common theme, that someone is being enthroned beside "the LORD" (Yahweh). So that is a very interesting thing, and that creates this ambiguity that Jesus is somehow identified with Israel's *kyrios*, Israel's Lord (Yahweh); that is something we see in the narrative. So, I mostly agree with what Bart is saying, but I think we need to consider some extra details in the story.

The other thing Bart does is to point out how the exalta-tion of Jesus has an affinity with the exaltation of other figures from antiquity, like Romulus and Enoch. And again, this is perfectly true. One thing I tell my students is that you cannot understand how Christianity is different from Greco-Roman religion until you first understand how they are similar. And there are genuine analogies and similarities. Certainly, if you read a passage like Acts 13:33–34, there is exaltation language [meaning], "This man Jesus has been exalted to divine status." We face questions: Is that all they believed? Was that the limits of their belief? Do they compact everything around that? Do they believe nothing more? That is what I'm not so sure about.

The other thing I have to say is this: I am not convinced that belief in the resurrection alone would make Jesus divine. I mean, if one of the other poor chaps who was crucified with Jesus was believed to have been raised from the dead, would they have worshiped him (cf. Luke 23:39–43)? Would they have concluded that he was enthroned with Yahweh, that we should now use the language of Isaiah 45 to describe him, that he held life and power, redemption, and the majesty of God in his hands? I don't think so. Because we know of stories where people were believed to have died and gone to heaven, *but they were never worshiped as divine.* A good example is the Testament of Job (4–5). Job's children die under a horrible earthquake. They go looking for the bodies. They can't find them. They don't infer resurrection; they say they have been assumed to heaven. But they don't start worshiping them or offering prayers to them, or that sort of thing. They have gone to recline in the bosom of Abraham [cf. Luke 16:22–26]. You know [*singing*], "Rock my soul in the bosom of Abraham," something like that. But they are not thereby divine. Similarly, in the Testament of Abraham (13), I think it is Abel who dies. He goes to heaven and becomes like the angels. He has a heav-enly transcendent status. But he is not worshiped or regarded as God. I will also contest your reading of Philo on Moses,

Bart. It is true. Philo says Moses becomes God, but he makes the emphasis that Moses is God *in relation to Israel* (*On the Life of Moses* 1.155–58). He has godlike power over Israel. In fact, Philo goes out of his way to specify that he is not God in the same way as the Father, because Moses does not have control over nature in the same way that Israel's God did. So, he has godlike power and status over Israel, but he does not seem to be exalted in the same sense as Israel's God who is the uncreated Creator (*That the Worse Attacks the Better* 161–62; *That Every Good Person Is Free* 43).

The second to last thing I would add is agreeing that Raymond Brown was a great scholar. I really like him. I have learned a lot from his works; but he is not the only show playing in town. There is another great critical scholar I like, John Knox. And I do not mean the Scottish reformer. I mean a scholar from the mid-twentieth century (1901–90). He argues that Jesus' preexistence is what the disciples inferred from his resurrection. So, that isn't something that developed later. He thinks preexistence is something they inferred from the resurrection because if Jesus has ascended into heaven, then in retrospect he must have descended in the first place. That could be the type of logic that is being employed.

The final thing I will say is this: I think Bart is completely right that the views of the Trinity did develop. They were contentious. The question was this: Whose way of telling the story is the most compelling and the most coherent? What explains both the biblical text yet as well explains believers' experiences? If you go through the text, then that really is the question: Which is the best way of putting it? If you read the Jesus' baptism story as a modalist, as Bart pointed out, it is ridiculous. It becomes a moment of divine ventriloquism. Jesus is talking to himself, doing his own voice from heaven. It might be a good vaudeville show, but it does not make good Christology. Similarly, the Great Commission in the Gospel of Matthew (28:18–20) tells us, "Therefore baptize them," and it has "Go in the name of the Father, Son, and the Holy Spirit." No one would baptize in the name of a deity, a creature, and an impersonal force. It would not make a lot of sense to do that. So, the question was "Which view had the most coherence and the best value at explaining their Scripture and their experience?" And Bart is correct that views of the Trinity developed from earlier views, but those other views were done in dialogue with Scripture, and the task is finding the best way of framing the debate. Yes, Arians, modalists, Docetists—they all looked to Scripture for their answer, yet the one view that did win over the majority, in the end, was [what came to be known as] the orthodox view. They said, despite whatever problems it has, it seems to be the way that has the most going for it in explaining the text and our experience and what we have learned.

Questions and Answers

Question #1: Dr. Ehrman, thank you very much for an excellent presentation and response to Dr. Bird. In *How Jesus Became God*, you follow John Dominic Crossan in rejecting the historicity of Jesus' burial; after citing Crossan, you conclude that "Roman practice was to allow the bodies of crucified people to decompose on the cross. . . . I have not run across any contrary indication in any ancient source."[50] So my question is this: if you run across Josephus in *The Jewish War*, which Crossan cites, you find where Josephus writes that typically in Judea, Jews were careful to bury their crucified before sunset. Furthermore, are you aware that in the chapter of his work that you cite, Crossan notes the first-century skeleton of a clearly crucified man? If you were aware of that ancient evidence, why do you say that you have not run across any contrary indication? If you were not aware of that evidence, how would you now account for it?

Ehrman: Thank you. Thank you. Yes, that's a good question. So, let me explain what's going on in my book. When I

---

50. Bart D. Ehrman, *How Jesus Became God: The Exaltation of a Jewish Preacher from Galilee* (San Francisco: HarperOne, 2014), 160.

earlier said that the empty tomb would not lead anybody to faith, what I didn't say is that *I don't think there is an empty tomb*. It's a rather long and complicated argument, which I'm not going to be able to give in one minute thirty-three seconds. But the reality is that every Roman and Greek source that talks about crucifixion, that mentions the facts, says that the bodies were left on the cross. They were left on the cross to allow the body to decompose. Because that was part of the punishment. If you think that you can cross the power of Rome, this is what will happen to you. You will be tortured to death, and you will be left on the cross to rot. And that's what Romans did. Yes, I am familiar with all the passages in Josephus and in other texts. When I said that there is no contrary evidence, I was saying that *in Greek and Roman sources*, there is absolutely no evidence to the contrary. Josephus gives two instances of people coming off the cross, but in those two instances the people were not dead. Romans did not care about Jewish law, in Palestine or anywhere else. They were Romans. They did not follow Jewish law. In Jewish law, if Jews had crucified people, they'd have to take them off the cross. If you want to see my fuller explanation, I actually deal with this passage in Josephus; go to my blog, because I give about a two-week answer to these questions, as they were raised by Craig Evans. I'm out of time.

Question #2: Dr. Ehrman, I've heard you explain before that we can't reliably say that the apostles have died for their faith, meaning historically. Is that because there's no documentation? Or the documentation was from a later date? Or because it was based on tradition? Does that apply to Peter or Paul?

Ehrman: Thank you. So the question is, do we know how the apostles died? The reason I've made this comment before is that all of you have probably heard that the disciples would not lie about the resurrection, because all of them were martyred for believing in the resurrection. That is commonly stated. And my view is that we don't know how the disciples died. And we don't know. How would we know? You might think, well, there must be records, right? Wrong. If you read through the book of Acts, which is about the apostles, most of the apostles have no role at all to play. There are a couple of martyrdoms. James is killed. Stephen is killed. Stephen, of course, was not one of the Twelve. Well, how were the others killed? We don't know. We don't start getting texts that talk about the death of the disciples until the late second century. These texts are recognized by everybody as legendary. If somebody says to you that the apostles all died for their faith in the resurrection, ask them what their source of information is, because they don't have a source of information. They say that because that's what they've heard. And if you ask the person they heard it from, what their source of information is, they won't have a source of information. We don't have actual stories of them being martyred until the late second century. We do have a reference to Peter and Paul being killed probably in Rome, in the book of 1 Clement, from the year 96 or so CE. But the writer doesn't tell us *why* they were martyred. Clearly, they believed in the resurrection, and clearly, they got martyred. So I assume it has something to do with that. The other disciples—we simply don't know about them because we have no records.

Question #3: Dr. Ehrman, is it correct to say that you believe Jesus' self-claims of divinity in the Gospel of John are merely late and are inventions? And if so, are there any passages in the Gospels that you consider to be factual? What criteria do you use in deciding what is factual and what isn't?

Ehrman: Good. Thank you. In the Gospel of John, Jesus repeatedly makes divine claims for himself, claims found only in the Gospel of John. Jesus says, "Before Abraham was, I AM." Thus he claims the name of God for himself. And the Jews know what he is saying because they take up stones to stone him to death. That's John 8:58–59. In John 10:30–31, Jesus says, "I and the Father are one." Once more the Jews took up the stones. So, Jesus tells his disciples that if you have "seen me," you have "seen the Father" (John 14:9). Therefore, in the Gospel of John, Jesus is claiming to be a divine being. There is no doubt about that. So the question is posed: Do I think these claims are late and legendary? And the answer is yes. I don't think that the historical Jesus went around saying, "I am God." As Michael himself pointed out earlier, Jesus did not go around saying, "I'm God." The Gospel of John is portraying Jesus as a divine being, and that Gospel is having Jesus call himself a divine being. But such language in the Gospel of John does not mean it historically actually happened.

Here's my view of it. If Jesus went around calling himself God, the way John portrayed it, that would be the most important thing to know about him, wouldn't it? I mean, what would be more important to know than that this man is calling himself God? That would be fundamentally important. If that's the case, why did Matthew, Mark, and Luke neglect to mention it? They just forgot to bring up that part, that he's calling himself God? How is that possible? It is a stunning silence.

Well, if I don't think those passages in John are reliable historically, do I think *anything* is reliable? Yes, of course. There are many things in the Gospels, even in the Gospel of John, that are reliable. And scholars use historical criteria to decide what is reliable. I absolutely think there is historical material in the Gospels, but I think that among that material, it is not Jesus' claims to divinity.

Bird: I will try to chime in just to remind people I exist. (*Laughter.*) I think the Gospel of John is a mixture of memory, midrash, and mysticism. That sounds a bit complex. I think there is a historical tradition in John, but it is being pushed through a very thick interpretive layer. So, what we get in the Gospel of John, even on the lips of Jesus, is not just the words of Jesus, not just the voice of Jesus, but sometimes the impressions Jesus made on his earliest followers are incorporated in the narrative. So, I think there is a historical tradition in John. Some say that John is historically worthless. I wouldn't go that far. But John is different than the Synoptics. I describe the Gospel of John this way: imagine you're going from New York's peak-hour traffic to Mardi Gras's traffic. It's just very different, what is going on.

Question #4: This question is for both of you. If you give a list of the Christologies that were on offer in the early church and you gave a list of modalism, adoptionism, separationism, and so on, do you both agree that one thing not existing anywhere in the early church would be a Christ mythicist view, where there is no human Jesus whatsoever, but there's some celestial or heavenly Jesus or something that we worship? You know, there is a modern school thinking there was a group that had a Christology like that.

Bird: If you mean some sort of early Jesus myth, à la mythicist view, no. When you get into some of the gnostic and esoteric literature, you do find something like Jesus being a cosmic aeon or something that's taken on some sort of human form or such. But maybe not in the precise sense for which you're looking.

Ehrman: I not only get an unkind reception from certain fundamentalists; I also get an unkind reception from certain mythicists, who get really upset with me. Atheists and agnostics who otherwise think they should like me, don't like me at all, and it's because I think Jesus existed. Right, so . . . (*Laughter.*)

Bird: Can I add on that?

Ehrman: Yes.

Bird: Even if Jesus existed, even if the early church had a high Christology, you can still be an atheist, but you can't be a stupid atheist. (*Laughter.*) It's going to be alright. I want to give you pastoral assurance. (*Laughter.*)

Ehrman: Right. Okay. So, I wrote a book called *Did Jesus Exist?*, which argues that, yes, Jesus *did* exist. Were there any early Christians who thought that Jesus did not exist? No! It's a completely modern invention. It's a kind of scary modern invention. You might not be familiar with this: there's a very loud voice on the internet now arguing that the historical Jesus is a myth, that he didn't exist. And I think that it's an awful view. I do think it's a stupid view, but there are people who subscribe to it.

Question #5: You said that Jews had no problem with deifying people, referring to them as being, you know, at the side of God and so forth, but in Mark 14:61–64 [cf. ESV], you have the high priest asking him, "Are you the Christ, the Son of the

Blessed?" And he says, "I am, and you will see the Son of Man seated at the right hand of Power, and coming with the clouds of heaven." Now, at no point does Christ say, "I am God," as you said earlier, but yet they all then immediately say, "We don't need any more proof; he's just blasphemed; we should kill him." So, if the Jews were at the point of wanting to kill Jesus for saying something like that, how were you saying also that they had no problem with people being deified otherwise?

Ehrman: Thank you. I'm not saying that every Jew was happy with every person who was thought to be God. In Mark's Gospel, the understanding is that Caiaphas and the Jewish council are upset that Jesus is apparently making some kind of divine claim about himself. So, that doesn't mean that they excluded everybody from making a divine claim for himself. This is talking about Jesus here. Moreover, Caiaphas and the council are not representative of all Jews. There is no doubt that Jews thought human beings. Enoch is worshiped as a divine being in the book of 1 Enoch. Philo calls Moses "God." There are other instances of this in Jewish literature: as I said, I have thirty-seven pages of the book on this, and I'm just scratching the surface. So, it's absolutely right that the council is upset with Jesus because they think he's making a divine claim, but that doesn't mean that all Jews were always afraid of deifying a human being.

Bird: I'll just add on that quickly. There's no question that there was a belief that certain figures, like Enoch, had been elevated to a certain status, had been assumed into heaven. Yet as the main issue, they didn't want that to transgress the orbit of Yahweh's authority or receive the worship, the monolatry, the worship that was exclusively meant to belong to the one God. My favorite story of Jews being allergic to worshiping a human being is that the Jews in Pella tore down images of Caligula. That event led Caligula to order that a statue of himself be put in the Holy of Holies [39–40 CE]. "If the Jews don't all worship my image, then I'll put my image in their very temple" [that desecration was aborted]. That to me shows Jews' really steep allergy to the worship of human figures. It may not be shared by everyone in the same intensity, but I think there is a crisp line separating the uncreated God from the creation.

Question #6: My question is for Dr. Bird. Dr. Ehrman brought up Acts 13—I think it was verses 32–34, or somewhere around there—a couple of times, and I assume you don't have an adoptionist interpretation of that passage. So, in two minutes, can you give us the non-adoptionist interpretation of that?

Bird: In hindsight, I probably should have said something about those texts. Acts 2 never mentions Jesus as becoming a son, so it's not adoptionist. If you're not made a son, you were not adopted. Yes, it does have an exaltation: the man Jesus is elevated to this great status. But that does not mean that's the only thing they believed. It doesn't mean that it cannot be married to preexistence or something else. The other thing in Acts 2, if you read the wider context, yes, there are things like preexistence going on, all sorts of things being said about Jesus. In fact, the main emphasis is not the status reversal of Jesus, but rather it is the epistemology: Israel needs to know that the man whom they crucified is the one whom God has made Lord and Messiah. In other words, the main point is that God has reversed the verdict that the Jewish leaders had made about Jesus. Now, when you get to Acts 13, yes, you have this same issue of Jesus' change in status, from human Messiah who was the Son of God, into this divine status. But a full-length citation of Psalm 2 does not an adoption make because you can find similar language in Justin Martyr and other places where it's not used in adoptionist fashion.

Ehrman: I think the key is the wording in that Acts 13 passage. So, Paul says that the promises were fulfilled: God fulfilled the promises by raising him from the dead. "You are my Son; today I have begotten you" (13:33). So, it's the point of that speech where he becomes the Son of God. Whether you want to call that adoptionism or not doesn't really matter to me. If you want to call it exaltation, like Michael, that's fine. If a being is exalted, that means they are raised to a higher level. They can't be already at that higher level prior to their exaltation: if so, they're not being exalted. How I understand the earliest Christology is that Jesus was put on a higher level. I'm not saying that that's a right Christology. I'm not saying it's a Christology that people ought to believe. I'm saying that was the original understanding of the Christians that later developed into other christological views.

Question #7: My question actually segues off of his. One of the words that keeps coming up is "begotten," especially in that passage, the phrase "begotten." So, I was wondering about adoption in Judaism and the terminology "begotten." Is there any precedent in any other texts or any other sources where we see specifically "begotten" and the other language tied to adoption within the Jewish tradition?

Bird: Not in the Jewish tradition, but in the Greco-Roman tradition, the first person to talk about the gods being begotten and immutable is Plutarch.

Ehrman: Thank you.

Bird: It's true, Bart.

Ehrman: That's a great question. So, "begotten" is language for a male who brings forth a child. Obviously, the male doesn't become pregnant, but the male makes the female pregnant, and she brings forth. Thus it's a tricky thing with God, because if God's a male, how does he give birth? But that's the idea, that he gives birth. Were you asking about the Jewish tradition specifically?

Questioner: Yes, in the Jewish tradition, because the earlier Synoptic Gospels would have been set mainly in a Jewish tradition.

Ehrman: Yes, I understand; what I would argue is that the Synoptic Gospels are influenced not only by Jewish traditions but also by Greek and Roman traditions. The Gospels are written in Greek, for example. They're not written in Aramaic, the language of Palestine. They're written in Greek. In Greek and Roman circles, there was a very common idea that a god could bring forth a divine human. And so, in Greek and Roman mythology, for example, sometimes a god will make a woman pregnant, and the child will be both human and divine. That's where Hercules comes from. Hercules is a divine man because Jupiter gets the woman pregnant, and her child then is a son. And so you think, "Well, yes, but you wouldn't find that in Jewish circles." Except that you do. In Genesis 6, for example, where the sons of God looked upon the daughters of men and saw that they were beautiful, they came down and cohabited with them, and their offspring were these giants who were roaming the earth (6:1–4). This is borrowing into that view that you have: here you have heavenly beings who make an earthly being pregnant. And so, you don't have anything quite like the begotten language in the first century, none that I know about, but it certainly stands in both the Greek and Roman and Jewish traditions at some points.

Bird: Michael Peppard has a good discussion of begotten language in the early church; see his book *The Son of God in the Roman World*.[51] I recommend that you read the book.

Question #8: Dr. Ehrman, do you believe that Jesus is perfect God, perfect man, all the way God, all the way man, the hypostatic union of Christ? Do you believe that he died for all of your sins on the cross and for all of our sins; that it was efficacious, paid for our sins, made us just; and then that he rose from the dead, and went [to give] each and every one of us that precious free gift of everlasting resurrection life; that he took care of our death problem with his resurrection; that he took care of our sin problem when he died on the cross; and that his blood washed us white? Do you believe that? If you don't believe all that, maybe you believe some of it. Elaborate please, thank you.

Ehrman: No, I don't believe any of that. I did believe that when I was in high school. When I was a fifteen-year-old, I accepted Christ as my Lord and Savior and committed my life to him. After high school, I went to Moody Bible Institute, which was at the time a bastion of fundamentalist Christianity; I was very rigorously involved with my faith and wanted to devote my

51. Michael Peppard, *The Son of God in the Roman World: Divine Sonship in Its Social and Political Context* (Oxford and New York: Oxford University Press, 2011).

life to Christ and his kingdom. And I was completely committed to the Bible as the inerrant revelation of God. I had a personal relationship with Jesus as my Lord and Savior, and I was like that for years. As I studied the Bible more, I began to realize, reading it in the original Greek and in the original Hebrew, that in fact it simply wasn't an inerrant revelation. I wanted to believe it was, but I started finding discrepancies. I found out how people resolve these discrepancies. I got to a point where I just realized that some of these differences cannot be reconciled and are just contradictions. And I had to decide: Am I going to go where I think the truth is leading me, or am I going to stay where I feel more comfortable? And I decided I really had to go where I thought the truth was leading me. I ended up becoming a liberal Christian. I was still a faithful Christian. I was a pastor of a Baptist church for a year. I was still actively involved in ministry.

Eventually, the reason I left Christianity altogether was unrelated to my scholarship. It's because I simply no longer could believe that there was a God who was active in a world where there is just so much pain, misery, and suffering; where a child, an innocent child, starves to death every five seconds. I realized that I just don't believe it anymore, so I became an agnostic about twenty years ago. So, no, I don't believe any of that.

Bird: I became a Christian about twenty years ago. I don't know if I'd quite put it the way the gentleman put it. But I grew up in a very non-Christian background. Growing up, everything I knew about Christianity I learned from Ned Flanders. He was the only pastor I ever knew. And I thought all Christians were just moralizing geriatrics. And then I actually met some, and they introduced me to the good news of Jesus, and I just prayed one night to receive Christ, and that was the moment I left the matrix. (*Laughter.*) I could go on to talk about things, but people do not often ask me why I became a Christian and why I am still a Christian; it's for one simple reason. I believe in the utter worshipability of Jesus. That's all I have to say on that.

Question #9: My question is about the charge of blasphemy in Mark, in particular in Mark 14 [cf. 14:61–65]. And it's for Dr. Ehrman, but I'd like to hear what both of you think. I thought I'd heard you saying that Jesus doesn't claim to be divine in the earlier Gospels, in particular in the Gospel of Mark; yet we were just looking at the account of the trial before Caiaphas, where Caiaphas asks, "Are you the Christ, the Son of the Blessed?" And Jesus says, "I am; and you'll see the Son of Man seated at the right hand of power and coming on the clouds of glory." And then they charge him with blasphemy. There Jesus is quoting Psalm 110 and Daniel 7. So, my question is this: Is Jesus claiming to be divine there? If he's not, then why do they charge him with blasphemy in the context of a question about his identity? And second, why does he quote Psalm 110? This is part of the same question because it ties into preexistence. In Mark 12 and Mark 14, he quotes Psalm 110, which is the one psalm in the Old Testament that says, "Before the daystar, . . . I have begotten you" [110:3 New Catholic Bible]. So, isn't preexistence implicit there? Here are two questions in one, I hope. Sorry. (*Laughter.*) My main question is this: Is he making a divine claim there? And if not, why the blasphemy charge (Mark 14:64)?

Ehrman: That's a complicated question, and it really would take a detailed exegesis, which would obviously take a long time to do. I think it's one of the more confusing passages in the Gospel of Mark, because technically speaking, Jesus does not commit a blasphemy. The chief priest asks him, "Are you the Messiah, the Son of the Blessed?" And Jesus says, "I am." Now, that's not a blasphemy. He's saying, "Yes, I am the Messiah." There's no blasphemy in claiming to be the Messiah. The Messiah was just the future king of Israel, and so that's not a blasphemy. And then he says, "You will see the Son of Man coming on the clouds of heaven." That's also not a blasphemy. Jesus is simply referring to Daniel, claiming that you (the high priest) are going to see what Daniel predicted in Daniel 7:13–14. But then they cry out, "Blasphemy." So, what's the blasphemy? There are a number of theories about this. One theory that I don't accept is that when Jesus says, "I am," he's claiming the divine name for himself. I don't think so because the words for "I am" simply mean "yes." Are you the Messiah? Yes, I am the Messiah. It's not claiming the divine name. It's just how you say yes. So then, if that's not the blasphemy, what is the blasphemy? I think you need to understand that for Mark, for Mark himself, the author of this Gospel, Jesus is the Son of Man. Jesus is coming back in glory. Jesus has been exalted to the right hand of God, and he's coming back as the judge of the earth. It's not that some anonymous son of man is coming. *Jesus* is coming. Mark thinks that's what Jesus is. So, when Jesus says you will see the Son of Man, Mark requires you to think that Jesus *is* the Son of Man. The high priest knows that he thinks that. Thus the high priest thinks he's claiming to be the Son of Man, and so he calls out, "Blasphemy." So, is it a divine claim? Well, yes, somewhat. I mean, it is, kind of. But it's not like Jesus saying, "I and the Father are one." Sorry, I'm out of time.

Voice from the audience: It's the invention of Mark.

Ehrman: Yes, of course, it's the invention of Mark. Look, we don't know; there's no way we can know what happened at the trial of Jesus before Caiaphas. This is Mark's account. So, I'm talking about the historical Jesus. We don't know what happened at the trial before Caiaphas. How would we know that? Jesus would have known.

Question #10: Dr. Ehrman, in your book you said the authors of the Synoptic Gospels did not believe that Jesus was preexistent. Those same authors, though, believed that Jesus was the Son of Man, and that the Son of Man figure in Judaism of the Second Temple period was a preexistent figure. So, I'm wondering how you put that together: Why did they not believe that Jesus was preexistent if they believed that he was the Son of Man?

Ehrman: I don't think Second Temple Judaism had a single belief about anything. Different Jews believed different things. Some Jews thought that the Son of Man was a being who was preexistent; other Jews thought that the Son of Man was some human advanced to be the Son of Man. For example, in the book of 1 Enoch, the character Enoch becomes the Son of Man. He wasn't always the Son of Man: he becomes the Son of Man in 1 Enoch. In Christian thinking, Jesus became the Son of Man. For Matthew and Luke, he becomes the Son of Man. All you need to do is read Matthew and Luke's birth narratives. It's rather clear, especially in Luke: when Jesus is conceived, when the Holy Spirit makes Mary pregnant, that's when Jesus comes into existence. There's not a word about his preexistence.

Question #11: In the Gospel of Mark, when Jesus claims to have the authority to forgive sins (2:5–10), or when Jesus stills the storm (4:37–41), or when he says that the Son of Man is lord of the Sabbath (2:28), is the author of Mark trying to imply that Jesus is the God of Israel?

Bird: I think he's definitely edging into that category. Just treat the dynamics of the story, as when we read, "Who can forgive sins but God alone?" (Mark 2:7). Thus by forgiving sins, and claiming the authority to do so, it does edge in that direction. The idea of a human forgiving sins made sense so long as you had a priest in the temple. You could offer a sacrifice, and the priest would pronounce absolution or the efficacy of the sacrifice. But this seems to be independent of that. So Jesus is offering this temple sort of forgiveness, but independent of the normal institution. If you look at the dynamics of the Markan story, it seems that Mark at least understands this as a claim to offer something that [only?] God was known to give: forgiveness. Now, there may be places in other texts where humans can forgive sins. There is a text in the Dead Sea Scrolls where a Jewish exorcist forgave sins [The Aramaic Prayer of Nabonidus: 4Q242]; there may be something like this going around. But the dynamics of the Markan story seem to say that Mark thinks Jesus is [seen as] usurping [or claiming] a divine prerogative for himself.

Question #12: Dr. Ehrman, I'm curious: you said that one of the reasons the disciples might have come to think that Jesus was divine was because of the empty tomb and the postmortem

appearances. You expressed your view that Jesus was never buried, or if he was, that he was buried in a shallow grave. How
do you explain the postmortem appearances, and specifically
when Paul claims that he appeared to over five hundred people
at one time?

Ehrman: I don't think that Jesus was buried by Joseph of
Arimathea on the day of his crucifixion, as is recorded in the
Gospels, because that would've been not just unusual; so far
as I know, that would also have been unique. In Greek and
Roman sources, they always talk about people who were crucified not being buried. The Christian belief later was that Jesus
was raised from the dead on the third day; it was very precise:
it was on the third day. The empty-tomb story emerged as a
way of showing that, on the third day, the tomb was empty,
even though in our earliest sources, Paul does not mention an
empty tomb.

What do I think about the appearances? So, Paul certainly
says that he had a vision of Jesus, but he doesn't tell us exactly
what he saw. Did he see a human form that he identified as
looking like Jesus? He doesn't tell us that. What he says is that
the resurrected body of Jesus is completely different from the
current body. In 1 Corinthians 15 he is attacking Christians
who say that the dead are not going to be raised in the future.
Paul says, "Yes, they are going to be raised in the future." Possible objection: "Well, what kind of body are they going to be
raised in? How can you imagine somebody being raised from
the dead?" So Paul has to answer this. Paul says, "It's like a
seed." You put a seed into the ground, and what grows from it
doesn't look like a seed. When you plant an acorn, the thing
that grows from an acorn doesn't look like a giant acorn: it's
an oak tree. Jesus' body before his resurrection was as different
from what came later as an acorn is to an oak tree. So we don't
know what Paul saw. But he saw something that he absolutely
identified as being Jesus raised from the dead.

What did the 500 see? We have no idea. Who were the 500?
We have no idea. Paul says there were 500. There is no account

of this in any of the Gospels, which is really strange. You would think that if stories were floating around about 500 people seeing Jesus, then that would be something you would want to point out in your narrative. But there's no narrative about that.

Is it possible that 500 people saw something that they interpreted as the resurrection of Jesus even if Jesus wasn't raised from the dead? Is that possible? Now apologists argue all the time that if 500 people saw Jesus, he must have really been there because you cannot have a mass hallucination. This is an argument that I run across all the time, that you cannot have a mass hallucination. The apologists who argue this are always very conservative evangelical, or fundamentalist, Christians. The people who argue this do not think that the blessed Virgin Mary ever appears in public today. We have reports of hundreds of people at the same time seeing the blessed Virgin Mary. So do you think that happened? If the answer is no, and you don't think the blessed Virgin Mary really appeared, then you think mass hallucinations are possible because they're reported. They're extremely well documented, much better documented than the appearance to the 500. So, I don't know what to think about the 500 except that apparently a large group of people saw something that they interpreted as Jesus.

Question #13: I would like to know about Paul's change of life from a Benjamite, from a Pharisee of the Pharisees: How do you explain his abrupt change, his complete turnaround from going house to house and taking Christians out of their houses and killing them, stoning them, and then his complete change into the apostle to the Gentiles (Acts 7:58–8:3; Phil. 3:4–6)? How do you explain that? And also, what about Peter's confession at Caesarea Philippi, how Peter, a rough fisherman, changes and says, "You are the Christ, the Messiah" (Mark 8:29)?

Ehrman: I think there's a very clear explanation for these transformations: both men believed that after his death Jesus appeared to them. They believed on the basis of something they saw and/or heard, that Jesus had been raised from the dead, and that completely turned their lives around.

BART EHRMAN: CONCLUSION

Let me just summarize my views about the topic for you once more and then end with an exhortation. My basic case in my book *How Jesus Became God* is as follows: I don't think that Jesus called himself God during his public ministry. I personally don't think Jesus imagined that he was God. He wasn't God: he was *God's prophet*. He was the one whom God had sent to proclaim the coming kingdom of God, which was soon to arrive, within Jesus' own generation. Jesus was not calling himself God. Certainly his disciples did not think he was God during his life; they couldn't even figure out how he could be the Messiah during his life. In the Gospels, at least—especially Mark's Gospel, our first account—they are clueless; yet later they came to say that Jesus was in some sense divine. Why is that? Because they came to believe that Jesus had been raised from the dead. Their belief in the resurrection is what led to their understanding that Jesus was God. Without the resurrection, that would not have happened. If Jesus had died and simply disappeared, nobody would have thought he was God. The turning point was the belief in the resurrection, which came because some of the followers of Jesus saw him afterward—or at least they *believed* they saw him afterward. But they knew he wasn't still there with them [as before]. So they wondered:

"Well, if he came back from the dead, where is he?"

"He's up in heaven."

"What happens when a person's taken up to heaven? What do they become?"

"They become a divine being." The earliest Christians thought that Jesus became a divine being at the resurrection, and once they started that belief, they started thinking more and more [about who Jesus was], and eventually they started thinking that Jesus was God, that Jesus had always been God, and eventually they came to say that Jesus was the God who was the creator of the world and that he was one with God the Father.

Those are later developments. They're not what Jesus thought and not what his disciples thought during his lifetime.

I know a lot of people are reluctant to agree with that because it stands contrary to what they've always thought about Jesus himself during his life.

So let me end with my exhortation: Whether you agree with me or not, I really would encourage all of you to at least be willing to think, and not to be afraid to change your views about something, even if it's something really important to you. I encourage you to be willing to go wherever you believe the truth is taking you. Thank you very much.

MICHAEL BIRD: CONCLUSION

On the topic of ancient monotheism—what was it called?—we've heard a lot about the nature of historiography and its relationship to faith. We've heard a lot about Jesus as well. Just to give my final summary thoughts and my two cents, I believe Jesus acted with a sense of unmediated authority. I believe he cited passages like Psalm 110 and combined that with the Aramaic idiom of self-reference to "a son of man" from Daniel 7, making himself out to be one of God's main agents in the eschatological kingdom that was dawning, so that in and through himself, God was becoming King. The new exodus of Isaiah was happening: the great moment of liberation and redemption was under way. He spoke in such a way that the line between divine agent and divine sender was somewhat blurred. But it was with the resurrection and with belief in his exaltation that he was regarded as being enthroned and installed as YHWH's vice-regent. I think we're in that tunnel period that Simon Gathercole spoke about; yet I think there were some moments of retrojection because they thought that if Jesus has ascended, maybe he then had descended in the first place; if he is the firstborn from among the dead, then maybe he's also the firstborn of all creation; if he has been given all authority on heaven and earth, then maybe he always had that authority; if he has been crucified for our sins, then maybe he is the Lamb who was slain before the foundation of the world. Through inferences like that, I think we see the genesis of Christology, both diverse and developing; yet we see something along that kind of action taking place. But as I said, the most important question you can get out of this forum, the most important thing you can do, is to answer Jesus' own question, "Who do you say that I am?" Thank you very much.

Further Reading

ROBERT B. STEWART

This brief bibliography is written by an involved nonspecialist in the field of New Testament studies and is primarily intended to be an aid to readers who are also nonspecialists. For the most part, I have included only English-language translations. The first section covers the "classic works" of Jesus research and thus is organized generally in the historical order of authors' first work in this field; the second section is organized in the alphabetical order of authors' names, then chronological for that author. Mostly I merely summarize the contents, but at times I offer some personal opinions. They are just that, my own opinions.

Classics of the Quest

Reimarus, Hermann Samuel. *Reimarus: Fragments.* Edited by
Charles H. Talbert. Translated by Ralph S. Fraser. Lives of Jesus
Series. Edited by Leander Keck. Philadelphia: Fortress Press, 1970.

Published in fragments in 1774–78, this book is generally seen,
post-Schweitzer, as the starting point in surveys of the Quest. It can
be fairly described as conspiratorial in some sense and significantly
influenced by deism.

Strauss, David Friedrich. *The Life of Jesus Critically Examined.* Translated by George Eliot. Edited by Peter C. Hodgson. Lives of Jesus
Series. Edited by Leander E. Keck. Philadelphia: Fortress Press,
1972.

Strauss wrote four books on Jesus. His 1835–36 book (2 vols.) has
been the most significant since in it Strauss is the first to write that
the category of myth rather than history better captures the essence
of Jesus' message. Influenced by Hegelianism, he criticized the

rationalism of J. G. Herder and H. E. G. Paulus. He lost his job as a result of this book. Had he written seventy years later, he would have become a celebrity rather than a pariah.

Renan, Ernst. *La Vie de Jésus*. Paris: Michel Lévy Frères, 1863.

The first modern biography of Jesus. Like many of his time, Renan thought that Jesus was very non-Jewish in his character, values, and message.

Kähler, Martin. *The So-Called Historical Jesus and the Historic, Biblical Christ*. Philadelphia: Fortress Press, 1964.

Originally published in 1892, this work questioned the capacity of critical methods to reproduce Jesus; it observed that the historical Jesus was not the Christ whom the church worshiped. He concluded that the project of writing a biography of Jesus was doomed to failure.

Harnack, Adolf von. *What Is Christianity?* London: Williams & Norgate, 1900.

Originally published in 1900. Presenting a good example of classic liberal Christology, Harnack argues that Jesus emphasized the imminent arrival of the kingdom of God, the fatherhood of God, the infinite value of the human soul, and the moral responsibility to keep the Great Commandment.

Wrede, William. *The Messianic Secret: Forming a Contribution also to the Understanding of Mark*. Translated by J. C. G. Greig. Cambridge: James Clarke, 1971.

Vitally important work, originally published in 1901. Like Schweitzer, he was highly critical of the Jesus research that appeared earlier, believing it to suffer from "psychological suppositionitis" that made Jesus malleable to the point that he could be anything to anyone. Insisting that Jesus never claimed to be Messiah, he inferred that the messianic themes in the Gospels were the theological creation of the early church. His thesis has been hugely influential with many since then.

Schweitzer, Albert. *The Mystery of the Kingdom of God: The Secret of Jesus' Messiahship and Passion*. Translated by Walter Lowrie. New York: Macmillan, 1950.

Far less well known than Schweitzer's later book, this 1901 work is Schweitzer's attempt to state briefly who Jesus really was. Jesus, according to Schweitzer, was an apocalyptic prophet/messiah who mistakenly proclaimed the imminent end of the world. Ironically, it was published on the same day as Wrede's *Messianic Secret*.

————. *The Quest of the Historical Jesus: A Critical Study of Its Progress from Reimarus to Wrede*. Translated by W. Montgomery. New York: MacMillan, 1968; reprint, Baltimore: Johns Hopkins University Press, 1998.

Originally published in 1906, this book is (wrongly) believed by many (who never read the book) to have ended the Quest. Insightful at times, always written in stunning prose. One of the truly influential books in twentieth-century theology and New Testament studies.

Bousset, Wilhelm. *Kyrios Christos: A History of Belief in Christ from the Beginnings of Christianity to Irenaeus*. Translated by John E. Steely. Nashville: Abingdon, 1970.

Originally published in 1913, this work serves as a classic representative of the history of religions school (*religionsgeschichtliche Schule*), according to which the New Testament in general and the Synoptic Gospels in particular are but one part of a much larger socio-historical phenomenon, namely, the evolution of Jesus from Jewish Son of Man to Gentile God-Man. Importantly, Bousset distinguished between Palestinian Judaism and Hellenistic Judaism and held that orthodox Christianity is the result of the church becoming predominantly Gentile.

Troeltsch, Ernst. *Religion in History*. Translated by James Luther Adams and Walter F. Bense. Minneapolis: Fortress Press, 1991.

Contains several essays from the first quarter of the twentieth century by one of the most significant thinkers in the philosophy of history, including "Historical and Dogmatic Method in Theology," in which Troeltsch lays out his three historiographical principles: (1) methodological doubt; (2) analogy; and (3) correlation.

Bultmann, Rudolf. *Jesus and the Word*. Translated by Louise Pettibone Smith and Erminie Huntress Lantero. New York: Scribner, 1958.

Bultmann's mature position on the relationship of Jesus to the Christian church and Christian orthodoxy. He is highly skeptical of

recovering the historical message of Jesus because "the early Christian sources show no interest in either [his life or his personality],
are moreover fragmentary and often legendary; and other sources
about Jesus do not exist."

————. *New Testament and Mythology: And Other Basic Writings*.
Selected, edited, and translated by Schubert M. Ogden. Philadelphia: Fortress Press, 1984.

This collection contains some of his most important essays, including "New Testament and Mythology," "Is Exegesis without Presuppositions Possible?," and earlier and later versions of "On the
Problem of Demythologizing."

————. *The History of the Synoptic Tradition*. Translated by John
Marsh. Oxford: Basil Blackwell, 1963.

Vitally important book that rightfully recognizes the importance
of understanding the nature of what was being taught about Jesus
during the period between Jesus and the written Gospels, and in so
doing goes a long way toward justifying form criticism and especially the criterion of dissimilarity. Sadly, in my view it misunder-
stands its primary subject.

Käsemann, Ernst. *Essays on New Testament Themes*. Studies in Biblical
Theology 41. London: SCM, 1964.

Contains the 1954 paper that launched the New Quest, "The Problem of the Historical Jesus."

Robinson, James M. *A New Quest of the Historical Jesus and Other Essays*.
London: SCM, 1959; reprint, Philadelphia: Fortress Press, 1983.

Robinson was the historian of the New Quest. This book is a good
introduction to the New Quest.

Significant Works on Early Christian Christology

Anderson, Paul N., Felix Just, and Tom Thatcher, eds. *John, Jesus, and
History*. Vol. 1, *Critical Appraisals of Critical Views*. Atlanta: Society
of Biblical Literature, 2007.

————, eds. *John, Jesus, and History*. Vol. 2, *Aspects of Historicity in the
Fourth Gospel*. Atlanta: Society of Biblical Literature, 2009.

————, eds. *John, Jesus, and History*. Vol. 3, *Glimpses of Jesus through the Johannine Lens*. Atlanta: Society of Biblical Literature, 2016.

Three impressive volumes featuring top scholars demonstrating what Johannine scholarship has to offer Jesus studies. A long-overdue contribution.

Bauckham, Richard. *Jesus and the God of Israel: God Crucified and Other Studies on the New Testament's Christology of Divine Identity*. Grand Rapids: Wm. B. Eerdmans Publishing Co., 2008.

This important volume includes Bauckham's earlier book *God Crucified: Monotheism and Christology in the New Testament*, plus several other related essays. Bauckham argues that Second Temple Jews were primarily concerned with the "divine identity," *who* God is, rather than monotheism, *what* God is; Bauckham holds that Jesus shares the divine identity of Israel's God. Importantly, Bauckham maintains that first-century Judaism allowed for the possibility of real distinctions within the unique identity of God rather than for intermediary figures between God and man, thus allowing for Christian belief in Jesus' deity.

Baum, Armin D. *Der mündliche Faktor und seine Bedeutung für die synoptische Frage: Analogien aus der antiken Literatur, der Experimentalpsychologie, der Oral Poetry-Forschung und dem rabbinischen Traditionswesen*. Texte und Arbeiten zum neutestamentlichen Zeitalter 49. Tübingen: Francke Verlag, 2008.

Important book that makes a compelling case for believers' memorization of the whole Jesus tradition. Sadly, it has not received the attention it merits for this alone since it also argues that there is no literary relationship among the Synoptic Gospels, which few have found convincing, to say the least.

Bird, Michael F. *The Gospel of the Lord: How the Early Church Wrote the Story of Jesus*. Grand Rapids: Wm. B. Eerdmans Publishing Co., 2014.

This work delves into questions concerning the motivation for written Gospels, how the Gospels came to be written (the process from oral Gospel to written Gospels), how truthful they are in what they record, and why the early church settled on four rather than one or more than four, as well as addressing standard issues such as the Synoptic problem and the genre of the Gospels.

Bowman, Robert M., Jr., and J. Ed Komoszewski. *Putting Jesus in His Place: The Case for the Deity of Christ*. Grand Rapids: Kregel, 2007.

Written for nonspecialists, this exceptionally clear book makes the case for the deity of Jesus based on the acronym of HANDS, according to which Jesus shares the *H*onors due to God, the *A*ttributes of God, the *N*ames of God, performs the *D*eeds of God, and shares the *S*eat of God's throne. A solid piece of evangelical scholarship, intentionally written in an easy-to-understand style.

Boyarin, Daniel. *The Jewish Gospels: The Story of the Jewish Christ*. New York: The New Press, 2012.

Boyarin argues that many Jews believed Jesus to be Messiah because his core teachings were not a break from Jewish beliefs and teachings. What later came to be known as Christianity was the result of politicians and religious leaders seeking to impose a new religious orthodoxy that was not part of what Jesus or the earliest Christians believed. Essentially this is a case for Christ without Christianity.

Burridge, Richard A. *What Are the Gospels? A Comparison with Graeco-Roman Biography*. Cambridge: Cambridge University Press, 1992.

Burridge, a classicist turned New Testament scholar, seeks to demonstrate that the four Gospels really are "biographies."

Capes, David B. *Old Testament Yahweh Texts in Paul's Christology*. Wissenschaftliche Untersuchungen zum Neuen Testament 2/47. Tübingen: J. C. B. Mohr, 1992; reprint, Waco, TX: Baylor University Press, 2017.

An important study focusing on key passages in the Hebrew Bible where *Kyrios* in the Septuagint renders the Hebrew YHWH and how those passages are applied to Jesus in Paul's letters. Capes concludes that, in at least some places, Paul identifies Jesus with YHWH and considers Jesus to be one with God.

Carroway, George. *Christ Is God Over All: Romans 9:5 in the Context of Romans 9–11*. Library of New Testament Studies 489. London: T&T Clark, 2013.

A revision of Carroway's dissertation, this work argues that the most sensible interpretation of Romans 9:5, when considered within rhetorical context of Romans 9–11, is that Paul intends to say that Jesus is divine in a way that equates Jesus with YHWH. Carroway's main concern is to answer the question of why Paul would apply *Theos* to Christ at this point in his Letter to the Romans.

Casey, P. Maurice. *From Jewish Prophet to Gentile God: The Origins and Development of New Testament Christology.* Louisville, KY: Westminster John Knox Press, 1992.

Casey argues for an evolutionary Christology in three stages. Stage 1, the earliest stage, centers on Jewish believers during Jesus' life and for 10–20 years afterward who honored him as both prophet and Messiah. Stage 2 (basically the ministry of Paul) is the result of the Gentile mission and the influx of Gentile believers into the church, which resulted in diversity as to customs and beliefs regarding the person of Jesus. Stage 3 is after Gentiles constitute the majority in the church and translate Jesus from Jewish human Messiah into Gentile God-Man.

Collins, Adela Yarbro, and John J. Collins. *King and Messiah as Son of God: Divine, Human, and Angelic Messianic Figures in Biblical and Related Literature.* Grand Rapids: Wm. B. Eerdmans Publishing Co., 2008.

Important book that bridges a great deal of history and multiple cultures to discuss how ancient Jews would have understood the Messiah as king, and more importantly as divine. Crucially, the authors argue that it would be very Jewish to think of Jesus as divine, but in a lesser sense than YHWH, and to give relative worship to him. Regarding preexistence, however, that could be no part of either Second Temple Judaism or the earliest Christianity.

Davis, Carl Judson. *The Name and Way of the Lord.* Journal for the Study of the New Testament Supplement Series 129. Sheffield: JSOT Press, 1996.

A serious investigation of both the New Testament and external sources from roughly the same time period as to what Christians between 50 and 90 CE were likely to have understood by the application of Isaiah 40:3 and Joel 2:32 to Jesus in the New Testament. It finds that there are no clear pre-Christian Jewish parallels because Christians redefined monotheism so as to include both God and Jesus.

Dunn, James D. G. *Unity and Diversity in the New Testament: An Inquiry into the Character of Earliest Christianity.* London: SCM, 2006.

Intended as a response to Walter Bauer, this book focuses upon whether there was such a thing as either orthodoxy or heresy in the earliest church, and in so doing seeks to answer two overarching questions (and many sub-questions): (1) In what ways was the early church unified? (2) In what ways was the early church diverse? A very ambitious attempt at answering some important and wide-ranging questions.

———. *Did the First Christians Worship Jesus?* Louisville, KY: Westminster John Knox Press, 2010.

A cautious investigation of whether or not the earliest Christians worshiped Jesus, intended as a respectful response to Larry Hurtado and Richard Bauckham. Though at many points Dunn agrees with Hurtado and Bauckham, he prefers to state that worship was directed to God *through* Jesus rather than *to* Jesus himself; Dunn insists that talk of devotion to Jesus be made in terms of Jesus with God rather than to Jesus himself as the object of worship. Throughout, but especially late in the book, there is a concern to guard against Jesus-olatry.

Edwards, James R. *From Christ to Christianity: How the Jesus Movement Became the Church in Less Than a Century*. Grand Rapids: Baker Academic, 2021.

An insightful analysis of the development and continuity in the Christian movement from Jesus to the middle of the second century CE.

Ehrman, Bart D. *How Jesus Became God: The Exaltation of a Jewish Preacher from Galilee*. San Francisco: HarperOne, 2014.

The work that inspired this book. Ehrman's thesis is that Jesus did not see himself as divine during his lifetime, but that belief in his divinity arose almost immediately after his disciples had visions of Jesus that they mistakenly interpreted as meaning that Jesus had been resurrected. According to Ehrman, the earliest Christians thought Jesus had been exalted by God to a divine status at his resurrection, but this belief quickly morphed into the idea that Jesus was God incarnate.

Garrett, Susan R. *No Ordinary Angel: Celestial Spirits and Christian Claims about Jesus*. New Haven: Yale University Press, 2008.

Well-written book that focuses on angels, and particularly on how Jesus is similar to and different from angels, intentionally written for those with a high view of Scripture, those who are skeptical about angelic claims, and those who, like the late Walter Wink, are rightfully concerned to understand how the "powers" are systemically at work in our modern world. A serious attempt to strengthen and correct contemporary understandings of angels by informing them as to how angels were understood in the ancient world.

Gathercole, Simon J. *The Preexistent Son: Recovering the Christologies of Matthew, Mark, and Luke.* Grand Rapids: Wm. B. Eerdmans Publishing Co., 2006.

A scholarly offering from a (now) significant scholar arguing that careful exegesis of the Synoptic Gospels reveals a Jesus who was aware of his preexistence. Particular attention is given to the "I have come" sayings and to christological titles: Messiah, Lord, Son of Man, and Son of God. At the heart of this monograph is the question of Jesus' preexistence, not his nature à la Nicaea.

Gieschen, Charles A. *Angelomorphic Christology: Antecedents and Early Evidence.* Arbeiten zur Geschichte des antiken Judentums und des Urchristentums 42. Leiden: Brill, 1998.

Study attempting to demonstrate that the angel traditions in Judaism played a significant role in the development of Christology, particularly with regard to how "Angel of the Lord" traditions were linked to YHWH, and later became linked to the resurrected and exalted Jesus.

Grindheim, Sigurd. *God's Equal: What Can We Know about Jesus' Self-Understanding in the Synoptic Gospels?* London: Bloomsbury, 2011.

Grindheim argues that Jesus implicitly claimed to be God's equal, particularly through his claims to inaugurate the kingdom of God, but also through his understanding of his actions.

Hahn, Ferdinand. *The Titles of Jesus in Christology: Their History in Early Christianity.* New York: World Publishing Co., 1969.

Building on the work of Bousset, Hahn further refines the binary distinctions of "Palestinian-Jewish" and "Hellenistic-Jewish" made by Bousset into "Palestinian-Jewish," "Hellenistic-Jewish," and "Hellenistic-Gentile," thus arguing for a threefold pre-Pauline church.

Hengel, Martin. *The Son of God: The Origin of Christology and the History of Jewish-Hellenistic Religion*. Philadelphia: Fortress Press, 1976.

This volume, a revision of his 1973 inaugural lecture at Tübingen, deals primarily with the question How could Jesus, who died a shameful death as a conspirator in about 30 CE, just twenty-five years later be conceived in Philippians 2 as a preexistent divine figure, who after his death was exalted to the right hand of God? In answering this question, Hengel addressed the pre-Christian meaning of "son of God" and how this term changed via the experience of the first Christians.

———. *Crucifixion: In the Ancient World and the Folly of the Message of the Cross*. Translated by John Bowden. Philadelphia: Fortress Press, 1977.

Concise exposition of the historical and practical details of crucifixion in the ancient world, setting it among other forms of execution, especially the forms that predate the New Testament period, and showing how scandalous the crucifixion was for Second Temple Jewish believers.

Higgins, A. J. B. *The Son of Man in the Teaching of Jesus*. Society for New Testament Studies Monograph Series 39. Cambridge: Cambridge University Press, 2005.

A close examination of significant "Son of Man" sayings in the Synoptic Gospels, concluding that Jesus expected vindication of his earthly mission after his death by receiving a status of exaltation in the presence of God and that the Son of Man Christology in the Gospels originated not in the creative thought of early Christians but in the preaching of Jesus himself.

Hurtado, Larry. *One God, One Lord: Early Christian Devotion and Ancient Jewish Monotheism*. 3rd ed. Edinburgh: T&T Clark, 1998.

Virtually a modern classic, this work, intended to correct the mistakes of Bousset, investigates the origins of religious devotion to Jesus by analyzing how the devotion given to Jesus in first-century Christianity was like and unlike patterns of devotion in the Jewish religious background of the first believers. I strongly recommend reading the third edition, which includes a significant preliminary section in which Hurtado addresses several objections from his critics.

———. *Lord Jesus Christ: Devotion to Jesus in Earliest Christianity.* Grand Rapids: Wm. B. Eerdmans Publishing Co., 2003.

A tour de force, Hurtado's magnum opus is a full-scale analysis of the origin, development, and diversification of devotion to Jesus in the first 150 years of the Christian movement; it finds that devotion to Jesus arose remarkably early, was lived out with a passion for which there is no analogy, and yet was still within a monotheistic framework.

Kreitzer, Larry J. *Jesus and God in Paul's Eschatology.* Journal for the Study of the New Testament Supplement Series 19. Sheffield: JSOT Press, 1987; reprint, London and New York: Bloomsbury Academic, 2015.

This revised dissertation seeks to understand Paul's eschatology through his implicit Christology. In particular, it intends to answer the question of how Paul conceived of Jesus' relationship to God, doing so by answering the question of how Paul got from "the day of the Lord / Yahweh" to "the day of the Lord Christ."

McIver, R. K. *Memory, Jesus, and the Synoptic Gospels.* Society of Biblical Literature Resources for Biblical Study 59. Atlanta: Society of Biblical Literature, 2011.

This monograph is especially concerned with pedagogy and eyewitness tradition, thus taking into account the population and longevity of first-century Palestinian Jews; McIver finds it probable that even using standard-form critical assumptions on dating, a significant number of eyewitnesses were still living when the Synoptic Gospels were composed.

Moule, C. F. D. *The Origin of Christology.* Cambridge: Cambridge University Press, 1977.

Conservative book arguing that the high Christology of the New Testament is *not* the result of an evolutionary development by which a Palestinian rabbi is elevated, under the influence of Hellenistic savior cults, to the status of a divine lord, but rather represents only the development and exposition of what was there from the beginning.

Newman, Carey C., James R. Davila, and Gladys S. Lewis, eds. *The Jewish Roots of Christological Monotheism: Papers from the St. Andrews Conference on the Historical Origins of the Worship of Jesus.* Leiden: Brill, 1999.

Seventeen methodologically diverse essays from a stellar group of scholars, addressing specifically how devotion to Jesus in the first two centuries is a manifestation of Jewish monotheism. This volume represents some fruit of the Divine Mediator Figure Group of the Society of Biblical Literature.

Papandrea, James L. *The Earliest Christologies: Five Images of Christ in the Postapostolic Age*. Downers Grove, IL: InterVarsity Press, 2016.

A survey of the primary christological approaches available in the first few centuries of Christianity, compared and contrasted, along with some commentary on orthodoxy and heresy in the early church. Gnosticism is clarified by categorizing the different gnostic schools of thought according to their Christology, and the various Christologies are connected to their respective historical proponents and documents.

Peppard, Michael. *The Son of God in the Roman World: Divine Sonship in Its Social and Political Context*. Oxford and New York: Oxford University Press, 2011.

Sophisticated and careful study of the concept of sonship in the first-century Greco-Roman context in which the New Testament documents were written.

Smith, D. Moody. *John among the Gospels*. 2nd ed. Columbia: University of South Carolina Press, 2001.

Immensely helpful book on the relationship between John and the Synoptics; it also brings out much of the history of how New Testament scholars have addressed the question.

Stuckenbruck, Loren T. *Angel Veneration and Christology*. Wissenschaftliche Untersuchungen zum Neuen Testament 2/70. Tübingen: J. C. B. Mohr-Siebeck, 1995.

In a revision of his Princeton doctoral dissertation, Stuckenbruck argues that early Jewish Christians and other Jews allowed for veneration of angels but not for the worship of angels, thus maintaining a strict and rigorous monotheism.

Taylor, Vincent. *The Formation of the Gospel Tradition*. London: Macmillan, 1935.

A fair-minded introduction to form criticism (*Formgeschichte*) in English. Taylor correctly understood that the stories of Jesus had been edited and were representations reshaped for theological reasons having to do with the needs of early Christians. This book dispelled many fears about form criticism while at the same time critiquing some of its excesses (especially Bultmann's overestimation of the creative power of the community).

Theissen, Gerd, and Dagmar Winter. *The Quest for the Plausible Jesus: The Question of Criteria.* Translated by M. Eugene Boring. Louisville, KY: Westminster John Knox Press, 2002.

An expanded version of Winter's dissertation, which was supervised by Theissen, this work is a critical history and critique of the criterion of dissimilarity; it results in a call to replace the criterion of dissimilarity with the criterion of plausibility, which assesses both *contextual* plausibility and the plausibility *of later effects* together.

Tilling, Chris. *Paul's Divine Christology.* Wissenschaftliche Untersuchungen zum Neuen Testament 2/323. Tübingen: Mohr Siebeck, 2012.

Substantial work that asks how best to understand Paul's Christology in light of his Jewish belief in God; it asks where there is evidence, one way or the other, for understanding Paul's Christology with respect to the question of Jesus' divinity.

Zetterholm, Magnus, ed. *The Messiah in Early Judaism and Christianity.* Minneapolis: Fortress Press, 2007.

A concise collection of essays on messianism as variously understood and presented in pre-Christian Jewish traditions, the Synoptic Gospels, Paul, rabbinic literature, and postapostolic Christianity.

Index

CPSIA information can be obtained
at www.ICGtesting.com
Printed in the USA
LVHW030916131022
730395LV00002B/3